COURTS OF MANORS

OF BANDON AND BEDDINGTON

1498 - 1552

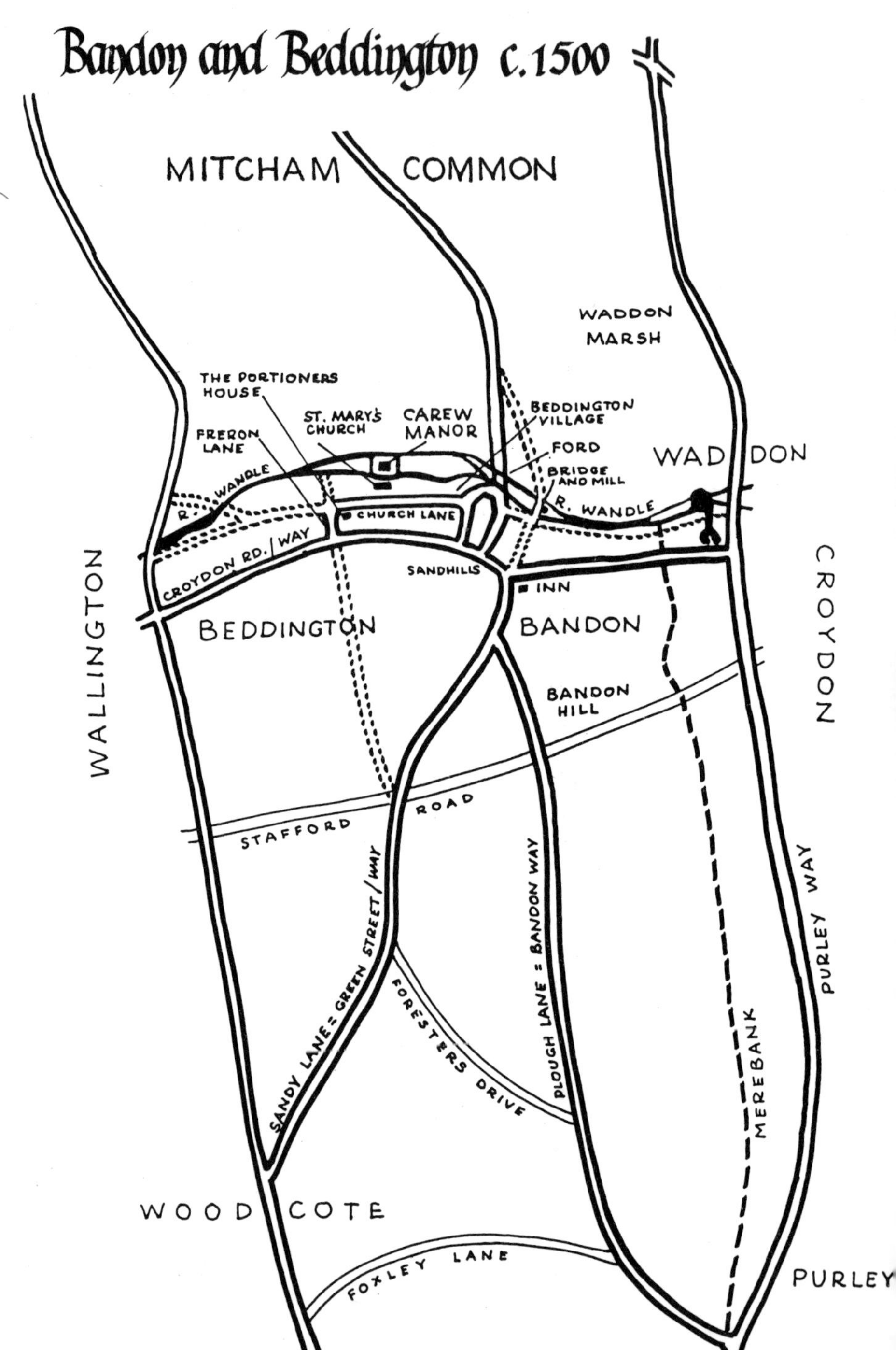
Bandon and Beddington c.1500
MITCHAM COMMON
WADDON MARSH
THE PORTIONERS HOUSE
ST. MARY'S CHURCH
CAREW MANOR
BEDDINGTON VILLAGE
FRERON LANE
FORD
BRIDGE AND MILL
WADDON
R. WANDLE
CHURCH LANE
CROYDON RD./WAY
SANDHILLS
INN
WALLINGTON
CROYDON
BEDDINGTON
BANDON
BANDON HILL
STAFFORD ROAD
SANDY LANE = GREEN STREET/WAY
PLOUGH LANE = BANDON WAY
PURLEY WAY
FORESTERS DRIVE
MEREBANK
WOOD COTE
FOXLEY LANE
PURLEY

COURTS OF THE MANORS OF BEDDINGTON AND BANDON 1498 – 1552

Transcribed and translated
by
Hedley Marne Gowans

Edited by
Michael Wilks & Jennifer Bray

London Borough of Sutton Libraries & Arts Services

First Published 1983

London Borough of Sutton Libraries & Arts Services
Central Library, St. Nicholas Way, Sutton, Surrey
Tel. 01-661 5050

ISBN 0 907335 08 X

Cover: Shirley Edwards

Printed and bound in Great Britain by
Anchor Brendon Ltd
Tiptree Essex

INTRODUCTION

This edition of the only surviving manor court roll for the 'lost' Surrey village of Bandon, together with fragments from neighbouring Beddington and other places connected with the Carew family, has been the work of many hands. But no one will deny that it is pre-eminently the work of Mr. Hedley Gowans of the Beddington, Carshalton and Wallington Archaeological Society, who first undertook the major task of transcribing the roll and providing a translation. It is essentially the fruit of his endeavours which is presented here. If Mr. Gowans fathered the enterprise from its inception, then the maternal role, so to speak, should be credited to Miss Jenny Bray of Birkbeck College, London, who not only checked and revised the texts against the originals, adding in some additional items in the process, but also carried the main burden of preparing the typescript for publication. Mr. Douglas Cluett may justly claim to have acted as godfather, and the editors' warmest thanks go to all the local studies staff at Sutton Central Library, and to Dr. R. B. Robinson and his colleagues in the Surrey Record Office at Kingston, for their constant helpfulness and apparently inexhaustible patience. We must also more formally record our gratitude for permission to publish the roll material from the County Record Office and the Public Record Office; and we must acknowledge our indebtedness to the London Borough of Sutton Library Services and to the Beddington, Carshalton and Wallington Archaeological Society, whose generous help has made publication possible at all. As will quickly become obvious, two other people, both well known to the public as the leading authorities on the early history of Beddington, have in different ways made a vital contribution to the preparation of this book. Mr. Ronald Michell's recent study of *The Carews of Beddington* (Sutton, 1981) is both a major addition to the history of the area and necessary background readin for the court roll itself. Mr. Keith Pryer deserves a special mention. He first drew attention to the existence of the roll, and he has already done a considerable amount of work on it. Some evidence of this has appeared in his discussion of *The Beddington Portion* (Beddington, Carshalton and Wallington Archaeological Society Occasional Paper No.2: 1973/74 which contains a wealth of information about Beddington during the Tudor period. Needless to say, neither of them should be held responsible for the less well founded remarks and suggestions about medieval Bandon and its neighbours which follow.

The bulk of this volume consists of the records o the sessions of the Bandon manorial court held during the reigns of Henry VII and Henry VIII between March 1498 and January 1531, a series of twenty-nine courts normally held annually, but here spreading over a tota of thirty-three years. There are also the records of two later meetings of the Bandon court in the reign of Edward VI, for April 1549 and October 1552. Although the corresponding Beddington manorial court sessions were held on the same day as the Bandon courts - and we may guess in the same place,[1] the Great Hall of

[1] The phrase used for both Bandon and Beddington courts, *curia ibidem tenta*, has been translated as 'a court held there': but it probably means no more

Carew Manor in Beddington Park - only three of these are included (January 1519, March 1528, April 1549). These are all to be found together on the roll now preserved in the Surrey County Record Office at Kingston. The previous history of the roll is obscure. Its existence appears to have been unknown until 1960, when a pupil at Clifton College, Bristol, brought it to a member of the College staff. It was then handed to the Bristol City Archivist, who passed it on to the Surrey County Archivist. The roll had been cut into sections, seemingly at an early date, and this presumably helps to explain why so many court records are missing. Some additional material is now in the Public Record Office (reference SC2/204/34), and covers the years 1545-6. This probably includes all the Bandon (March 1545, April 1546), Beddington (March 1545), and Beddington View of Frankpledge (June 1545, June 1546) courts held during the last two years of Henry VIII. Again there is no accounting for the survival of the material in this particular fashion. The seizure of his estates by the crown after the execution of Sir Nicholas Carew in March 1539 seems to have had no effect on the court rolls, which were still at Beddington at the time,[2] and, to judge from

than that the court met in the same place as on the previous occasion. Manor courts were often held in the hall of the manor house, but not necessarily so. Examples of meetings held in churches or in the open air under a large tree are known: the location was usually determined by custom. See further H.S. Bennett, Life on the English Manor (Cambridge, 1937), p.203. On the other hand the difference in names of those summoned to attend, and the case of April 1549 when a Bandon court was held but a Beddington one could not take place, show that the two manors were treated as separate entities, at least in a formal sense, even if the business deriving from the two areas was not strictly segregated.

[2] T. Bentham, *History of Beddington* (London, 1923),

the inclusion of the 1549/1552 courts, the records remained there until at least the end of the period of royal sequestration of the Carew manors.

Despite their incompleteness, the Bandon court records cover certain key dates in the history of the Carews. One does not of course know whether the Carews presided personally over their own local courts or preferred to delegate this duty to their stewards c bailiffs, whom one would expect to live in the manor concerned. But if they normally attended the courts, our volume opens in March 1498 with what may well have been the first appearance as a knight of Sir Richard Carew (who had succeeded his father James Carew at the end of 1492). Richard had been knighted on the battlefield at Blackheath on 17 June 1497 after assisting Henry VII to put down a revolt by Cornishmen protesting against heavy taxation. But some indicat: that Sir Richard did not attend many of the earlier courts may be found in the change after 1501 from the phrase 'Curia Ricardi Carew Militis ibidem tenta' to a mere 'Curia ibidem tenta': Sir Richard became Sheriff of Surrey in 1501, and subsequently Governor c Calais in 1509. No court is shown for 1510.[3] His

p.8: the inventory compiled by the first crown administrator, Sir Michael Stanhope, lists the rolls c the manor together with Froissart's *Chronicles* and Gower's *Confessio Amantis*.

[3] The apparent absence of a court in 1506 can probably be accounted for by the recording of two courts in 1505, 27 March and 17 September. The scri failed to realise that a whole regnal year elapsed between August 1505 and August 1506, so that after (correctly) dating the 27 March 1505 session to 20 Henry VII, he made the court on 17 September 1506 relate to 21 Henry VII instead of 22 Henry VII as it would by that time have been. In the same way the second 1511 court on 28 September was probably held i 1512, another year for which there appears to be a break: it ought to have been dated 4, not 3, Henry

name appears only sporadically after 1501: in 1508, 1514 and 1519-20; whilst for a period of four years, 1515-1518, the courts either never met at all or the records of them have been lost. Sir Richard Carew died on 18 May, two months after the session of the 1520 court (5 March), and was buried in the new family chapel in Beddington Church. He was succeeded by his son, Sir Nicholas, aged about twenty-five. Nicholas too had been appointed Sheriff of Surrey and Sussex in the previous year, and had already been associated with his father in the governorship of Calais. Knighted by 1517, he was not only Keeper of Greenwich Park, but a courtier who was usually required to be in close personal attendance on Henry VIII. Indeed he entertained his monarch at Beddington on two occasions, in 1519 and again in 1531. As Master of the King's Horse from 1522, employed on various foreign embassies, and during the 1530s protector of both Anne Boleyn and then her successor as queen, Jane Seymour, Sir Nicholas Carew 'was never far from the court'.[4] Even though he is known to have been in Beddington on numerous occasions, it is still odd that the Bandon and Beddington manorial courts are always described (in a way which was never true of his father's courts) as being courts of Sir Nicholas himself right up to the end of the series in 1531. Seven years later Sir Nicholas fell victim to the system of family alliances and political intrigues which he himself had manipulated so brilliantly in first promoting and then

VIII. This lack of familiarity with the system of regnal years, together with some peculiar Latin and spellings, might indicate that the court recorder was a local figure rather than a member of the Carews' political staff.

[4] R.A. Michell, *The Carews of Beddington* (Sutton, 1981), pp.27f.

destroying Anne Boleyn:[5] he was duly beheaded on Tower Hill on 3 March 1539. The Carew estates were confiscated, and as a result the Bandon and Beddington manorial courts of 1545-6 and 1549 were now described as courts of Henry VIII and Edward VI themselves. In practice the estates had been farmed out for management by royal officers (*firmarii regis*),[6] and in 1552 they were granted to the Lord Chamberlain, Thomas, Lord Darcy, who held his first court[7] at Bandon - and the last in this volume - on 8 October in that year. His third son, Sir Arthur Darcy, was already in possession of the manors of Woodcote, Sutton and Epsom by virtue of his marriage to Mary Carew, the late Sir Nicholas' third daughter. Little more than a year later, in January 1554, the new queen, Mary Tudor, restored 'the manours of Beddington, Ravensbury Bandon and Norbury in the County of Surrey and all other lands and heridytaments in the same County ... also the manours of Ebbysham [Epsom] and Sutton ... and the manours of Bansted and Walton on the Hill, with lands in Charlewood and Horley' to Mary's brother, Francis Carew.[8]

The formulae and procedures of the court records appear at first sight to be dauntingly technical, but the entries on the roll do for the most part follow a fairly simple prescribed form. The basic purpose

[5] See further E.W. Ives, 'Faction at the Court of Henry VIII: The Fall of Anne Boleyn,' *History*, lvii (1972), pp.169-88; *Faction in Tudor England* (Historic Association: London, 1979), especially pp.17-20.

[6] See below, p.65.

[7] 'Prima curia': below, p.78.

[8] Michell, *Carews*, p.42, who points out that Franc Carew also purchased the estates from Lord Darcy. Francis had been a member of the Queen's household fro before 1550.

of a manorial court roll was to record the land holdings in the manor, and the events and decisions which affected the running of the estate. The court would also deal with other properties which were part of other manors but where the tenant had a feudal obligation to pay suit of court at this particular place. Decisions were not determined according to the arbitrary wishes of the lord of the manor, but in accordance with the traditional custom of the manor, which the lord was expected to accept as much as he imposed it on his tenants. The determination was made by a jury of adult male tenants, who were summoned to do this on the basis of their knowledge of the custom of the manor. The assessment of payments due to the lord - the rent for land holdings and the penalties for breaches of discipline - were similarly fixed by custom, and were assessed by two assessors or 'affeerers' from amongst the tenants. Strictly speaking there were two different types of manorial court. The leet court with a view of frankpledge was theoretically derived from a royal grant enabling the lord to deal with offences which would otherwise require the attention of the royal judicial system. It was supposed to meet twice a year; it too needed a jury to be sworn; and it was dependent upon the frankpledge system by which a group of perhaps ten or a dozen households, or even the whole hamlet or village, formed a tithing, and the tithing was held corporately responsible for the good conduct of its members and obliged to present breaches of the law to the court for judgement. The court baron on the other hand was supposed to be concerned with the seigneurial rights of the lord, dealing with changes in tenancies, general administrative matters, and petty misdemeanours against the lord's jurisdiction. Courts baron were also supposed to meet every three weeks, but such frequent meetings can have left them little enough to do on each occasion. By the fifteenth century the Bandon court was meeting only annually, and it is not clear whether the lord of the manor of Bandon ever did have the right to hold a view of frankpledge in the way that the Beddington lord clearly did. Certainly by the end of the medieval period it was normal in practice to combine the various functions of the courts into the same session, even if the different kinds of business were still recorded separately, and the Carews seem to have made no distinction between the two types of manorial court. It is an interestir point that when the Carew estates were in the hands o the royal administrators in 1545-6 this distinction wa made at Beddington, and courts with a view of frankpledge[9] were held separately from the ordinary r of manorial courts.

The typical court opened, like a modern committe meeting receiving apologies for absence, with the *essonium*, the presentation of essoins or excuses for non-attendance. The tenants who were present first paid homage (*fidelitas*) to the lord and recognised th dues owed for their land holdings; and then they, as the homage (*homagium*), were sworn in to give evidence about those tenants who were in default. They then brought forward the first list of those in mercy (*misericordia*) for failure to fulfil their feudal obligations - owing suit at the manor court, doing fealty, paying rents and reliefs - and these were dul amerced or penalised by the appropriate fine. Since many of the defaulters were people who obviously live in London rather than locally, this was probably a formality, and was followed by an informal arrangemen under which there was a periodic settling up, usually

[9] See below, pp.68-70 and 73-5.

by an attorney. Thus Nicholas Burton of Fulham eventually sent his lawyer to pay his dues in 1509, although his son Thomas, who succeeded him in 1511, seems to have been equally recalcitrant about settling up.[10] Whilst the estate of Robert Morley, first complained about in 1503 - and despite a settlement by his widow Alice (who sent a chaplain to clear matters up in 1521) and another attempt to settle the debt by Alice's heiress and her husband, Dorothy and William Wylde, five years later - was still the subject of further amercements during the 1540s and 1550s when it had been purchased by Sir Roger and Lady Elizabeth Copley.[11] The amount due from each tenant was entered on the roll above the names of the people concerned - 'super eorum capita' (although for convenience it is shown alongside the name in the present text) - and the total sum due in fines written in the margin. When the tenant made default and admitted the obligation to pay, there was no problem. But if the tenant failed to do this, the bailiff would be ordered to distrain (*distringere*) the culprit by seizing whatever was needed to clear the debt.

[10] See below, pp.20-9.

[11] The estate was a substantial one, consisting of a capital messuage, an area of land called Lockyers, and another of fifty acres known as Dogges. In 1503 the house is described as being 'now in dairy' (*modo in deiaria*), although the meaning of this remains unclear: see below, p.15. The Copleys also purchased a half share of the lands attached to the manor of Stone Court, Carshalton, from Henry Gainsford in 1544: *Victoria County History: Surrey*, iv.184; D.L. Powell, *Court Rolls of the Manor of Carshalton* (Surrey Record Society, vol. ii, no.8: London, 1916), p.viii. The difficulty of enforcing manorial jurisdiction is discussed by Bennett, *Life on the English Manor*, pp.219-20. For a fuller description of the manor court process see here at pp. 20-3 and chapter 8 *passim*; and there is a convenient setting out of the difference between the leet court held for the view of frankpledge and the court baron in Powell, pp.xi-xiv.

The second main concern of the court was to record changes in land holdings and to extract the appropriate dues from new tenants. Where the property had been sold, which was classed as an *alienatio*, only the normal feudal dues were still payable. But where it had been inherited following the death (*obitus*) of the previous holder, or the heir came of age and took possession of his inheritance, the incomer was required to pay the lord a fine or heriot (*heriettum*), usually his best animal such as an ox or a horse or its equivalent, for each tenement. Again the bailiff was required, when necessary, to distrain for the debt. But a heriot was not payable, as the court roll solemnly spelled out in 1503, where the holding was subject to the *ius accrescendi*, according to which the survivor of another (in this instance Helen, widow of John Payn), or the remaining member of a group, inherited the land directly without the need for there to be a reversion to the lord of the manor and the recognition of a new tenancy.[12] After this, a further list of amercements dealt with offences against the good order of the manor lands, mostly 'outdoor offences' (*poena foris*): misuse of the fields, mostly by putting out cattle at other than the predetermined times, cases of trespass, damage to trees, roads and watercourses, and a great variety of similar misdemeanours. For instance in 1511 John Watersale (a name of ill-omen indeed!) was charged not only with cutting down one of the lord's elms, but also with possession of a ferret, which he had presumably been using to poach rabbits, and which the bailiff was required to seize.[13] In most cases it

[12] See below, p.17.

[13] See below, p.28.

was left to the bailiff to take the usual action to deal with the culprit, although occasionally a formal ordinance (*praeceptum, ordinatio, foret actio*) would be recorded, and there are many instances where the roll stipulates a day (*dies*) by which some customary manorial function had to be performed, such as the appointment of a shepherd, the erection of additional sheepfolds, the putting down or abandoning of certain dogs which had been killing the lord's rabbits, or the ringing and licensing of the Bandon pigs.[14] In addition the Beddington view of frankpledge courts in 1545-6 also dealt with the appointment of manor officials (*electio officiis*), like the constable and the tithing-man (*decenarius*, i.e. the foreman or spokesman for the tithing or frankpledge group), who were then sworn in.[15] Finally the members of the homage group who had been acting as assessors (*affuratores*) testified on oath to the correctness of the penalties and proceedings, and the total amount levied in fines was added at the end of the record.

To publish all the material now known to survive from the Bandon and Beddington manor court rolls immediately raises and - it is hoped - will provide an answer to a question which has long perplexed historians working on the area between Croydon and Sutton in North-East Surrey: where was the manor of Bandon? Bandon does not feature, at least in directly identifiable form, in Domesday Book. According to Domesday, after

[14] See below, pp.11-13: for pig ringing and licensing see also pp.10-11, 16, 51, 56, 72.

[15] See below, pp.70 and 75.

the Norman Conquest Beddington was divided into two manors, together with a third section which was technically part of the Kingston manor of Chessington.[16] For reasons which need not be pursued here (indeed the situation is complicated enough as it is), Domesday effectively treated Beddington and Chessington together as being part of the honour of Wallingford in Berkshire and then proceeded to divide them between two Norman magnates. Robert de Wateville, on behalf of Richard of Tonbridge, had two-fifths of Beddington and half of Chessington.[17] Miles Crispin had another two-fifths of Beddington, which was held for him by William FitzTurold, i.e. William son of Thorold. He also held the remaining Beddington fifth himself, although this was actually the other half of Chessington, 'whose land lay in Beddington'. For present purposes it will be enough to think in terms of three Domesday Beddingtons: the de Wateville Beddington, which included the church; the equally large Miles Crispin/FitzTurold Beddington; and the smaller Beddington area held by Miles Crispin himself. But it is not until a century and a half later that the first real opportunity to relate these different holdings to each other occurs with the tax assessments and returns for 1332.[18]

In 1332 the area which lay between Wallington on the west and Waddon to the east was classified, if

[16] *Domesday Book*: *Surrey* (ed. J. Morris: Chichester, 1975), 19.15; 29.1 and 2. For Chessington itself see 19.24.

[17] Richard of Tonbridge also held an area including woodland) in the adjacent royal manor of Wallington, *Domesday* 1.6, which may be an indication that his Beddington territory was in west rather than east Beddington.

[18] J.F. Willard and H.C. Johnson, *Surrey Taxation Returns* (Surrey Record Society vols xviii and xxxiii: 1922/23 and 1931/2), i.56-64 for Wallington Hundred.

only for taxation purposes, as three villages: Beddington, Bandon and Woodcote. Of these the 'villata de Bandon' was by far the largest, bringing in an amount almost equal to that of the other two villages put together - and it is very curious that by the end of the medieval period the much smaller village of Beddington had eclipsed the other two areas to such an extent that today the precise location of neither Bandon nor Woodcote is known with any degree of certainty. This is no doubt attributable to the constant acquisitions and centralising tendencies of the Carew family in Beddington. How far these areas were nucleated villages by the fourteenth century is also extremely doubtful. It is very likely that each of them had by this time acquired a recognisable village centre in proximity to a manor house. But these centres must have been surrounded by a number of widely dispersed hamlets and settlements, some of them forming subsidiary 'manors' of their own. As is the case in neighbouring Carshalton, the simplified Norman divisions of Domesday Book overlay a large number of separate Anglo-Saxon estates, which had begun to resurface by the thirteenth and fourteenth centuries as distinct entities, and one can expect the 1332 *villata* to consist in practice of several sub-manors in addition to the main manor bearing the name of the village itself. Beddington is a case in point, with half a dozen properties valued by the assessment at more than two shillings each.

The most valuable and so presumably the largest of these 1332 Beddington holdings was possessed by Simon Roce and was assessed at ten shillings, although the entry offers no clue as to its character and whereabouts.[19] One may guess that it covered the

[19] Op. cit., i.56. There is a holding for Henry Roce at Woodmansterne, i.59.

long gentle slopes of the Downs reaching southwards from the centre of Beddington towards Woodcote, or perhaps more probably the flat acres north of the river Wandle which became the modern Beddington Sewage Farm. But we do not know. Nor can anything be usefully said at present about John Lemman, who had a holding valued at three shillings. But in between Roce and Lemman on the scale of assessments there are two other estates which at once introduce names already familiar in the history of Beddington. The third largest property in 1332 was held by Thomas Corbet (at 3^s2^d), and according to the account given by the *Victoria County History* this represents the demesne of the de Wateville section of Domesday Beddington and included Beddington Church.[20] It can therefore be taken as the area around St. Mary's Church at Beddington Park, including the site of Carew Manor and the land on which the medieval village of Beddington lay immediately east of the church. It was held by the de Wateville family until the end of the twelfth century:[21] but from then on it escheated to the crown and was granted out to a succession of royal servants for the next 150 years. Two Thomas Corbets, father and son, both officers of the King's Household, had Beddington by royal grant between 1302 and 1338. But in 1345 this estate was granted to Sir Richard de

[20] The advowson of the church was given by Sybil de Wateville to Bermondsey Priory in 1159: *VCH*, iv. 169. Since the advowson was subsequently connected with the manor of Huscarls, this argues for a close relationship between Huscarls and Home Beddington.

[21] *VCH*, iv.169-70: by 1196 the crown had seized the lands of Ingelram de Funteneys, who had married Sibyl de Wateville. But the de Watevilles continued to hold land at Carshalton, Coulsdon and other local places until well into the thirteenth century: see *The 1235 Surrey Eyre* (ed. C.A.F. Meekings: Surrey Record Society vol. xxxi: Guildford, 1979), i.252-5.

Willoughby, and his wife Elizabeth, whose daughter Lucy aided the amalgamation of the Beddington properties by marrying Sir Thomas Huscarl at some point before 1348.

Sir Thomas Huscarl had the second largest land holding (6^s8^d) at Beddington in 1332, and was a member of another royal service family which had had possessions in Beddington for over a century before this. King John is recorded as making a grant of land at Beddington belonging to William Huscarl in 1215, and the family can be traced through from there to the 1370s.[22] In 1369 Sir Thomas Huscarl died, and his wife Lucy (de Willoughby) is said to have remarried to Nicholas Carew, who bought out the other Huscarl heirs in 1380-1. By this time however the Carews themselves had been connected with Beddington for half a century, and already in 1349 William and Nicholas Carew had acted as trustees for the Huscarl estate. In 1352 the latter, Nicholas Carew, leased the de Willoughby manor for life, receiving it in fee in 1363, and so effectively became the lord of the manor of Beddington from then onwards.[23] Meanwhile another of the major holdings of 1332, the property of St. Thomas' Hospital (assessed at 2^s6^d), has been identified with the so-called Freres Manor. This, including lands in Wallington and a watermill on

[22] *VCH*, iv.172-3. During the tenth and eleventh centuries housecarls were king's men, i.e. military retainers of the royal household to whom the king made grants of land in return for their services, a system which seems to have been common to both the Anglo-Saxon and Scandinavian monarchies: it may be relevant to note that c.920 Edward the Elder had seized the episcopal manor of Beddington to use for this purpose. There was a house and estate called Huscarls at Ingatestone, Essex, during the 1380s.

[23] See Michell, *Carews*, pp.6-14, for details.

the Wandle at Hackbridge,[24] had been created in 1220/1; but was reabsorbed into Beddington by Nicholas Carew in 1379.[25] In the course of the fourteenth century Beddington and the Carews became almost synonymous terms.

By this period most castles and manor houses either stood in close proximity to a parish church (as a great many still do) and tended to treat the church more as the lord's family chapel than as a general local building; or else these residences had acquired their own private chapels and oratories, serviced by a priest appointed as a family chaplain. From the beginning the Carews would have been able to make use of Beddington Church for their own requirements, since it seems reasonably certain that the medieval Home Beddington manor house was a building, probably moated and fortified, alongside St. Mary's Church on the south bank of the Wandle, on the same site as that now occupied by Carew Manor.[26] The house and lands of

[24] In 1359-60 the manorial court of Carshalton heard complaints that the Master of the Hospital of St Thomas at Southwark had caused flooding at Hackbridge by diverting water onto the common land of the manor: Powell, *Court Rolls*, pp.2-3, 6-7, 22-3. St. Thomas' Hospital was attached to the Cluniac Priory of Bermondsey. During the eighteenth century the Shepley estate at Hackbridge, which included a number of water mills, was said to have been 'anciently a religious house subject to the Abbey of Bermondsey': James Edwards, *Companion from London to Brighthelmston* (Dorking, c.1789), ii.24.

[25] A.W.G. Lowther, 'A Recently Discovered Early Charter (c. A.D. 1220-21) granting land etc. at Beddington and Wallington to the "New Hospital of St. Thomas the Martyr at Southwark",' *Southwark Archaeological Collections*, 1 (1949), pp.168-9. But note that in 1332 there was a Stephen Frere holding land at Carshalton: *Surrey Taxation Returns*, i.59.

[26] Michell, *Carews*, pp.22, 79. Nicholas Carew's will of 13 October 1387 was made out 'at the Manor House at Beddyngton'. All the Carews were buried in the church.

Beddington Huscarls, however, traditionally lay north of the river along the road which has since become Hilliers Lane.[27] The probability that this is correct is strengthened by the depositions made by a group of Wallington and Beddington villagers during the hearings of an inquisition into the value of the Beddington rectory in 1472: they testified that ' on the north part of the said church /of Beddington/ there are situate two hundred acres of land vulgarly called Huscarls Fee.'[28] It is not therefore surprising that in 1348 Sir Thomas and Lucy Huscarl obtained a licence for a chapel in their own manor house[29] which implies that Huscarls was sufficiently distant from Beddington Church for the ecclesiastical authorities to sanction a private chapel, even if it was desired as much as a mark of independence and social status as an indication of genuine need. At the same time this distance between Home Beddington and Beddington Huscarls does not justify the *Victoria County History*'s assumption that Huscarls must therefore represent a different part of the Domesday division of Beddington, and that it can be identified with at least some of the lands assigned to Miles Crispin.[30] On the contrary the evidence of the 1332 assessments is direct testimony that Huscarls was a subsidiary 'manor' of the

[27] Michell, *Carews*, pp.6, 12.

[28] See K.A. Pryer, *The Beddington Portion* (Beddington, Carshalton and Wallington Archaeological Society Occasional Paper no.4: 1973/4), p.22.

[29] Pryer, *Beddington Portion*, p.10, citing the second volume of the episcopal register of William Edendon of Winchester (Hampshire Record Office, A1/9), f.16a.

[30] *VCH*, iv.172, on the grounds that Huscarls was part of the honour of Wallingford: but, as already stated, all of Domesday Beddington comes into this category.

demesne manor of Beddington, and any attempt to argue otherwise introduces quite unnecessary complications. We shall probably not go far wrong if we think that the three divisions of Domesday Beddington relate directly to the three villages or manors of 1332: Beddington, Bandon, and Woodcote. This triple division then remains a standard formula for the rest of the medieval period. Our court roll shows that Beddington and Bandon (if not perhaps Woodcote) were still regarded, however imprecisely, as separate manors well into the middle years of the sixteenth century. Only the use of the expression 'Bandon in Beddington' in 1612,[31] whilst indicating that Bandon was still a clearly recognisable place, suggests that the old medieval division was now on its way out.

The relationship of Huscarls to Beddington, confusing and irrelevant though it may appear, is in fact of considerable significance for the location of Bandon itself. The account given in the *Victoria County History* suffers from a number of defects. In the first place it implied that Bandon was a post-Domesday development, which mushroomed into prominence in the thirteenth and fourteenth centuries, and then vanished at the end of the Middle Ages as suddenly and abruptly as it began. Next, it argued that both Huscarls and Bandon were parts of the second Domesday holding, that of Miles Crispin and William FitzTurold, and that there must accordingly be a close relationship between them.[32] More recent scholarship has followed suit by suggesting that the manor of Bandon stood well

[31] Phillipps Collection MSS (London Borough of Sutton), i.2. The accounts of the Carew steward Thomas Mabson in 1568 and 1584 show the farms and rents of the manors of Beddington, Bandon and Woodcote being taken together: Bentham, *History of Beddington*, pp.37, 46-7.

[32] *VCH*, iv.174.

to the north of the river beyond Huscarls itself, and should be looked for on the fields of the sewage farm reaching over towards Mitcham Common.[33] Thirdly, by seeing Bandon as a mere portion of Crispin/FitzTurold Beddington, the *Victoria County History* reduces Bandon to relatively minor status, thereby making its 'disappearance' easier to accept - yet, as we have seen, in the earlier fourteenth century, before the great Carew takeover of Beddington, Bandon was not merely the equal of Home Beddington but had grown considerably larger by 1332. The total assessment for Bandon was 56^s2^d, as against 34^s3^d for Beddington and 33^s for Woodcote. One might expect Woodcote, much of which was apparently hunting ground, to bring in less than the more valuable cultivated land along the floor of the Wandle valley. Nevertheless we still need to think of Bandon as an area as big as Beddington, possibly even as big as Beddington and Woodcote put together. If we identify Beddington and Bandon *villatae* with Domesday's two larger divisions, they would in fact be roughly the same size. We should therefore remove Huscarls from the discussion, transferring it to what was originally de Wateville Beddington, so that Bandon can stand on its own as the successor of Crispin/FitzTurold Beddington. We are no longer tied to a connection with Huscarls, and Bandon is seen to have been a much larger and more important part of the area which is now modern Beddington than has generally been accepted. It would probably create a much more accurate picture if (as at Cheam) one thinks in terms of a West Beddington manor and an East Beddington manor. The former always enjoyed ecclesiastical precedence, and both manors

[33] Pryer, *Beddington Portion*, pp.5, 10, 28, 40; Michell, *Carews*, pp.6, 12.

were within the same parish of Beddington. But until the arrival of the Carews created a permanent shift in the balance between east and west, Bandon or East Beddington seemed likely to gain pre-eminence.

Scattered references to Bandon throughout the thirteenth century are enough to indicate its existenc as a place before 1200. The earliest known mention c the name comes in 1204, when Roger of Bandon was one c the recipients of a royal grant of land at Beddington which had formerly been held by the de Eys or Eyers family.[34] About 1220 Richard of Bandon was one of th witnesses to the grant of a 'manor' at Beddington to S Thomas' Hospital,[35] and between 1249 and 1262 Richard Bandon appears as a secular chaplain at Merton Priory. Although the largest landowner in the 1332 'villata de Bandon' was Richard Tymberdene,[37] the lord of the manc was probably Roger le Forester (assessed at $7^{s}1^{d}$) - with a John le Forester as one of the major tenants at neighbouring Woodcote. In 1349 Edward III granted, c rather confirmed, the royal manor of Bandon to Reginal [le] Forester (who seems to have acted as a royal escheator), his wife Matilda, and their son William: the reversion went to Edward, son of John Forester.[38]

[34] *VCH*, iv. 170. This makes it conceivable that Roger brought Bandon as a placename with him from elsewhere. But it is generally thought that Bandon means bean-down, like Be[a]nhill in Sutton.

[35] Lowther, *art. cit.* Richard of Bandon, priest purchased land in Wimbledon in 1235: *The 1235 Surrey Eyri* (Surrey Record Society, vol.xxxii: Guildford 19 no.273, ii.497.

[36] A. Heales, *Records of Merton Priory* (London, 1898), p.118: his allowance was to pass to his brothe Eudo for life, if Eudo survived him.

[37] At ten shillings (i.57): he also had other holdings at Mitcham, Bensham (Croydon) and East Cheam, i.61-2.

[38] *VCH*, iv.174; Pryer, *Beddington Portion*, pp. 10 and 12. Reginald le Forester had already acted as witness to a Coulsdon grant in 1338: *Chertsey Abbey*

That this was merely a confirmation is suggested by the fact that two years earlier in 1347 Reginald had acquired a licence for a chapel in his manor house.[39] The last member of the Forester family known at Bandon was Edmund Forester, who granted a piece of vacant land called 'Kolehawe' to William Bys in 1379: but the family's half-century tenure was enough to give Bandon a variety of alternative names - Foresters or Forsters or Fosters Manor - in subsequent centuries. Bys, citizen and fishmonger of London, had secured the manor itself by 1393, when he sold it to Thomas Remys. Remys in turn disposed of it in 1410 to a number of people, who seem to have been acting for Nicholas Carew, who is known to have had it by 1431.[40]

Despite the proliferation of manors and village communities, and the appearance of various separate chapels (Huscarls, Bandon, Wallington, and the notorious 'Beddington Portion'), the parish of Beddington remained essentially in its pre-Conquest form covering the whole area from Waddon to Carshalton. The episcopal inquisition of 1472, already mentioned above, into the value and extent of the Beddington rectory, derived out of a claim made in Chancery by the Carew

Cartularies, ii.1 (Surrey Record Society vol. xii cont.: Guildford, 1958), p.238. The same cartulary (p.150) also mentions a Jordan le Forester c.1190 at Waltham, but there may be no connection.

39 Edendon Register, f.13a. The similar grant of a license to Huscarls manor house the following year is unlikely to be evidence of imitation, but may indicate that the archdeacon of Surrey had made a tour of inspection in the locality and had taken action against unlicensed chapels. There was a *clericus* named Robert resident at Bandon in 1332.

40 *VCH*, iv.174. The sixteenth-century estate called Fosters at Chertsey derives from the family of Thomas le Forester who was at Chertsey in 1268: *Cartularies*, ii.1, p.lxix. Reginald Forester of Bandon in the 1340s seems to have had Chertsey connections.

lawyers that the incumbent of the Beddington Portion had an immemorial right to take tithes 'in certain lands and places called Bandon Field and Fosters Manor with their appurtenances, formerly the fee of Richard Huscarle' - a claim contested by the rector of Beddington on the basis that all tithes in the parish belonged to him. Leaving aside for the present any discussion of the precise nature of the Beddington Portion - except to note that it was clearly attached in some fashion to the Huscarl lands of some two hundred acres north of the river[41] - we can hardly ignore this quite astonishing assertion that Bandon manor had been part of the Huscarls property which the Carews had since inherited. Not only did the rector himself oppose this at the hearing, but he also brought forward witnesses who deposed as follows:

> John Gardyner of Wallington, in the parish of Beddington, where he had dwelt as a parishioner for 40 years then last and being 60 years of age and upwards and a Freeman ... Says he knows not when or in what manner it began and being interrogated in what part of the Parish aforesaid the said Portion exists says there is a certain Mansion with 20 acres of land belonging to

[41] See below, pp.xxxiv-vi, and Pryer, *Beddington Portion*, for a full discussion of the evidence. The portion appears to have been an area of land supportin a priest (who may have been a secular chaplain of Mert formed out of Huscarls, perhaps by a royal grant in 12 I have followed here the account of the 1472 inquisiti (Portionary Papers, Document A) given on pp.21-3, from which the quotation comes. The Carew involved in the case was technically Nicholas V (c.1463-after 1474), w was a minor - cf. Michell, *Carews*, pp.20-1, 118 - and claim was presented by Hugh Fenne (probably a relative Nicholas' mother, originally Margaret Fiennes) and William Essex, 'Guardians of the Lands and Heir under age'.

> the said Portion and the Portionary, which are situate on the south part of the Church aforesaid and on the north part of the said Church there are situate 200 acres of land vulgarly called Huscarls Fee, of which 200 acres of land the Portionary takes and has the Tythes arising therefrom ... Says that certain lands called Fosters Manor and Bandon Field are situate on the east part of the said Parish from which the Rector aforesaid ought to take Tythes for that they make one separate Demesne. Says that the said Rector always took without interruption the Tythes from the western part of the said land called Bandon Field as he now collects but the Tythes of the said lands situate in the part aforesaid the modern Portionary receives at present as if they were parcel of a certain Demesne called Huscarls ...

It is a statement which is not lacking in obscurities. Nevertheless it is immensely valuable evidence in one respect. Not only does it place Huscarls to the north of St. Mary's Church, but it also tells us that Bandon was a separate demesne which lay to the east of our modern Carew Manor area, forming 'the east part of the said Parish'. Furthermore, it implies that Bandon Field (which may be presumed to be one of the common fields of the manor) lay north of the river, but to the east of Huscarls' land - since the point at issue was that the rector of Beddington, who appears not to have taken tithes from Huscarls property, did begin taking tithes when he dealt with the western part of the field. There is also a hint that the field and the manor were some distance apart (as is the case in other local areas): the witness thought it necessary to make the point that Bandon Field and Bandon Manor should be treated together 'for that they make one separate Demesne'. The suggestion is that Bandon manor house was elsewhere, that is, to the south of the river.

References to Bandon Field in the court roll itself do little to help us to establish where it was.[42] On the other hand confirmation that Bandon reached towards Mitcham Common and the north-eastern part of modern Beddington may be thought to be provided by the complaints that various inhabitants of Mitcham were overgrazing Bandon Common or Heath with their sheep and cattle.[43] Similarly complaints against trespass by the vicar and other residents of Croydon,[44] and the possibility that the Eastlands

[42] Below, pp.26, 72; and 63 indicating that Bandon possessed more than one common field.

[43] Between 1522 and 1529 Richard Gylis, Thomas Webbe and Thomas Forman, all of Mitcham, were accused of offences on a common variously called 'Bandon comen' or 'communia vocata le Heth' (below, pp.45, 56, 58, 60-1; cf. p.54: in 1511 William Cogge cut down a large hawthorn on 'le Comyn Heth', p.28). A similar complaint relating to Bandon Common was made against Henry Kneppe in 1549: he too was probably from Mitcham, since there had been a Richard Knep of Mitcham in 1527 (pp.76, 55). Although dealt with by a Bandon court in 1524, another such case involving Beddington Heath suggests that that area was to the west of Bandon, since one of the accused, Richard Wryght, was from Carshalton, and another, John Stapyl[illegible] 'firmarius', had been selling wood in Carshalton in 1511: pp.48, 29, and see below p.6 and n.54 - both were accused together of cutting down trees in 1525 (p.51). In 1528 John Richebell of Wallington was als[illegible] accused of wrongful occupation of the heath (unspecif[illegible] p.57).

[44] See the complaint about Philip Rowlond, vicar of Croydon, in 1505 (below, p.23); and the charge tha[illegible] the Croydon carters John and Peter Bereman, Brown or Bronn Vanryggen, and Hans or John Pvirs were crossing the manor without the lord's permission in 1501-3 (pp 11, 13, 16). It is interesting to note some distinctly foreign-sounding names here.

abutted the lands of the archbishop of Canterbury,[45] would indicate that the eastern boundary of Bandon lay next to Waddon, one of the manors attached to medieval Croydon.[46] Reference to a Westland[47] would presumably relate to that part of Bandon adjoining Beddington on the opposite side of the manor. Bandon must also have included a section of the river Wandle, since it is known that there was a manorial water-powered cornmill,[48] and (at least in the early seventeenth century) Bandon Mill stood beside a pond upstream, i.e. eastwards, from Carew Manor.[49] Whether

[45] Below, p.29: the land was held by John Haccher, described as a collier or charcoal-burner of Croydon, and had previously been (the duke of ?) Norfolk's, pp. 34-5.

[46] For 'le Shott vocata Waddon Marke' see below, pp.15, 53; and for the possession of Croydon and (after 1390) Waddon manors by the archbishop of Canterbury see F.R.H. Du Boulay, *The Lordship of Canterbury* (London, 1966). The western boundary of the manor of Waddon coincided with the western edge of the parish of Croydon along the Merebank, which ran across the present Croydon Airport/Roundshaw site: L. Thornhill, 'A Croydon Back-Cloth: Some Little Known Estate Maps in Lambeth Palace Library,' *Proceedings of the Croydon Natural History and Scientific Society*, xvi (1977), pp.105-24 at p.112. Is there a reference to this in 1511 when John Hyller was charged (p.28) with cutting down oaks and nut trees 'super le Bank in Cullewylhawe'?

[47] Below, p.16. Note that Beddington manor also had a Westland, p.38: These are presumably different areas.

[48] The mill is mentioned in 1511 and 1546 (below, pp.29 and 72): the miller in 1502 was Thomas Mores (p.13).

[49] Phillipps Collection MSS (Sutton),i.3 contains a lease of Bandon Mill by Sir Nicholas Throckmorton-Carew of Beddington on 9 October 1613 to John Smythe of Beddington, miller. The mill was to grind wheat for use at Carew Manor as well as rye, and had a pond which neighbours were permitted to clear of mud, and

this offers a clue to the position of the manor house, which is often to be found in the vicinity of a manorial mill, must remain an open question. But it is very tempting to suggest that the well known Beddington corn and snuff mill in Wandle Road, with its pond reaching eastwards towards Waddon, and always inconveniently too far east of Carew Manor, does in fact mark the site of Bandon Mill.[50]

Equally problematical is the question of how far the manor extended south of the river. Mention of another common field called the Southfield[51] only leads to the query: south of what? But the existence of a Bourn Field[52] suggests one of those places which

the miller was to ensure that mud was not washed downstream to Sir Nicholas' orchards and lands. John Smithe was one of the millers who signed the Carew petition of 1610 against an attempt to draw water from the river: M.S. Giuseppi, 'The River Wandle in 1610,' *SAC*, xxi (1908), pp.170-91 at p.179.

[50] It is not clear whether the Bandon Mill of the previous note is to be identified with the Old Mill which gave its name to 'Oulde Mill Bridge and Howse' in Bandon and which features in a lease of 23 September 1612 by Sir Nicholas Carew to Jeremy Matthew a tailor of Bandon, Phillipps MSS, i.2. But Wandle Road bridge is the only old bridge known between Croydon and Beddington. Beddington is credited with four mills in Domesday (19.15; 29.1), two in each of its main sections; and in 1387 Nicholas Carew (d.1390) listed four watermills in his will: but the Carews did not have the manor of Bandon at this stage, and the Beddington mills may well have been downstream towards Beddington Corner. The established history of the present mill in Wandle Road only dates back to the eighteenth century, when it was a flour mill. It was sold and rebuilt in 1780-3 as John Williamson's snuff mill, subsequently becoming the well known Lambert family snuff mill, but returned to flour milling c.188[illegible] for the Wallis family of bakers, and was largely rebuilt during the 1890s.

[51] Below, p.79.

[52] Below, p.51.

are a common feature of the villages between Croydon and Cheam where streams from the North Downs periodically surfaced and ran down into the Wandle: one would expect a bourn to flow towards the river from the south. In contrast to the flat expanse of land north of the Wandle, the court roll includes names which might be thought more appropriate to the gentle slopes and rises of the modern Bandon Hill area. Thus in 1511 the Bandon court heard a complaint that the Worple ('le Worpyll') was being blocked by John Stapyll or Staple's ploughing: this is a common Surrey term for a hill road or bridleway,[53] and as the context suggests that it ran up to the Downs, perhaps turning towards Carshalton, it is reasonable to guess that it followed the line of the modern Sandy Lane to Woodcote - rather than going in the direction of Plough Lane across Roundshaw to Purley.[54] Plough Lane itself was probably part of a much longer road, including Beddington Lane and Hilliers Lane, called Bandon Way in a survey of 1514.[55] The Sand Hill[56] may be thought to be today's Sandhills at the northern end of Plough Lane. There is also a 'Leggerhill',[57]

[53] The earliest form seems to be *wapple*. The word is preserved in the modern placename Worplesdon (Domesday: *Werpesdune*, 18.3), and there are Worple Roads in Wimbledon, Epsom, Leatherhead, Staines and Isleworth.

[54] Below, p.29: Stapyll's offences included cutting gorse and furze on 'Le Down', which was then sold in Carshalton, and refusing to use Bandon Mill, perhaps because it was too far from Carshalton.

[55] As suggested by Pryer, *Beddington Portion*, p.40.

[56] Below, pp.8, 51. References to an oak growing 'in Sandels' in 1511, and in 1521 to land called Sundriche (pp.28, 44) may relate to the same place.

[57] Below, p.33: but note that Legger appears as a surname throughout the roll.

and an area of gorse and furze known as the Down or Sheep Pasture.[58] If little is to be gleaned from the numerous references to the sheep, pigs and horses which were kept on the manor lands, what would appear to be a rabbit warren[59] would again suggest an upland area. The Eastlands too had sufficient wood to make them attractive to a Croydon collier or charcoal burner,[60] which again might imply a more southerly setting for the area. We shall probably not go far wrong in regarding Bandon as a place which stretched southwards across the old Croydon Airport site at Roundshaw to meet up with Purley on one side and Woodcote on the other. In other words Bandon should be seen as East Beddington, taking its place as another of the long narrow strip-parishes so typical of the upper Wandle and forming part of a sequence running from Waddon through Bandon, Beddington West, Wallington, Carshalton and Sutton, to East and West Cheam - with both Wallington and West Beddington foreshortened to the south by the 'manor' of Woodcote lying athwart their downland sections.

Like this end of Bandon, Woodcote was a downland village with 'diverse and sundry sheepwalks and sheeproughs' and it also had a warren.[61] The court roll sees it as a well wooded place, whose trees and

[58] Below, pp.29, 79.

[59] Below, p.13.

[60] See above at n.45.

[61] *Surrey Feet of Fines*, 1509-1558 (Surrey Record Society, vol.xix, 1946, rpt. 1968), p.109, no.832: in 1556 Francis Carew purchased from Thomas Darcy the manors of Beddington, Bandon, Norbury and Ravensbury, which included forty houses, twenty farms, two watermills, 1,000 acres of land, 100 acres of water meadow, 2,000 acres of pasture, 500 acres of wood, 1,000 acres of heath and furze and a free warren in Woodcote and Beddington, and the advowson of Beddington church, and paid him £2,400.

hedges were a good but illegal source of firewood.[62] It had a settlement which now appears to be lost without trace, and included at least one sizable building which probably originated as a royal hunting lodge and, like almost everything else, was duly acquired by the Carews.[63] Whether or not it is correct to see Woodcote as the third (Chessington) part of Domesday Beddington, its early history follows a very similar pattern to that of the other two areas - a first mention between 1200 and 1208, followed by a series of sporadic references leading up to the list of landholders provided by the 1332 taxation returns. In the first decade of the thirteenth century a number of cases about disputed lands in the royal manors of Wallington and Woodcote were heard in the *curia regis*, and these featured Lucas 'de la Wdecot', together with Walter and his son and daughter-in-law, Baldric and Emma.[64] Baldric and his brother 'Graland de la

[62] Below, pp.10, 42. There are constant complaints about the way in which hedges etc. are broken down for firewood: e.g. pp.13, 16, 18, 21, 29, 44, 51.

[63] See the (undated) interrogation made on behalf of William Paire, defendant, to Elizabeth Burton, widow, in the Phillipps Collection MSS (Sutton), iv.1: '3. Did you know that the said Sir Nicholas Carew was in his life time seized in his demean as of fee of and in the Manors of Beddington and Bandon in the county of Surrey, and of and in diverse and sundry sheepwalks or sheeproughs thereunto belonging, Yes or No? 4. Do you not also know that the said Sir Nicholas Carew was likewise seized of and in one other capital messuage and warren of conyes which before appertaining in Beddington aforesaid commonly called or known by the names of Woodcott and the Old Lodge. And likewise of and in one other spectiall or severall /?/ sheepwalk or sheeprough belonging also unto his said messuage called Woodcott. Yes or No?' I am grateful for this reference to Mrs. Margaret Cunningham , whose forthcoming study of the history of Woodcote Hall , Wallington, contains a number of references to the early history of the area.

[64] A convenient reference list is available in K.W.

Wudecot' reappear c.1220 as witnesses to a Beddington charter,[65] whilst in 1223 the *curia regis* rolls list Alfred and Gilbert of Woodcote. Occasional sparse references during the remainder of the century are compensated for by the list of some fifteen principal tenants in the 1332 assessments.[66] These included the John le Forester already mentioned in connection with Bandon; and holdings of similar value ($3^s6\frac{3}{4}^d$) are recorded for William 'de Cherlewode', William Snell, and Roger 'ate Grene'. The last named, however, if taken together with Walter 'at the Green' (2^s6^d), would compare in amount to the largest holdin of all, that of Ferandus of Spain (5^s6^d), whose name suggests that he may well have been a merchant, mercenary or royal servant, one of the numerous foreigners who were at court in connection with Englis trade, diplomacy and warfare in Gascony, Castile, and Portugal during the fourteenth century. But from her on any real evidence for a village at Woodcote abruptl vanishes, despite sixteenth-, seventeenth- and eighteenth-century reports of substantial remains, which were inevitably taken to be those of a Roman city.[67] There is now mention only of some sort of

Muckelroy, 'Woodcote or Woodcote Warren, once a City according to Tradition,' *SAC*, lxix (1973), 37-45, who suggests that a new village was established by Henry II and was abandoned again after the Black Death in 1349.

[65] Lowther, *art. cit.* They also appear in the *Chertsey Abbey Cartularies*, ii.1, pp.220-1, as witnesses to a Carshalton charter of 1230/35, togethe with William the Marshall of Woodcote and John the Marshall of Carshalton, also T/homas/ Huscar/l/e. Grayland was still alive in 1241: p.xcv; and S. de la Wodecote appears on a Coulsdon charter of perhaps c.1300, p.246.

[66] *Surrey Taxation Returns*, i.56.

[67] To illustrate the prolonged debate initially

house or hunting-lodge. In 1392 there is a record that land in Carshalton had previously been held by one Richard 'atte Kechyn (kitchen?) de Wodecote'.[68] We can only speculate whether some more numerous settlement existed then, or whether plague or Carew enclosure depopulated the area. The Beddington and Bandon courts roll, as already said, seems to confine itself to mention only of trees and hedges at Woodcote. In 1550 Sir Arthur Darcy, brother-in-law to Francis Carew, used a fallen log from Woodcote to make joists for 'the Lodge in Woodcott'.[69] Two years later Sir Arthur's father, Thomas, Lord Darcy, was granted the rabbit warren at Woodcote together with the Beddington and Bandon manors.[70] But beyond that there is little more to be said at present.

generated by Camden's statement that Woodcote was a little wood on top of a hill which contained many flint walls (or wells) and other signs of a populous town, which he identified with Noviomagus, mentioned in the *Antonine Itinerary*, see G.J. Copley, *Camden's Britannia: Surrey and Sussex* (London, 1977), pp.21-2; John Evelyn, *Diary* (ed. E.S. de Beer: Oxford, 1950-5), iii,221; John Aubrey, *Natural History and Antiquities of the County of Surrey* (rpt. Dorking, 1975), ii.151-9; and *Monumenta Britannica, I-II* (ed. J. Fowles and R. Legg: Sherborne, 1980), pp.448-9, 462-3; Daniel Lysons, *The Environs of London* (London, 1792), i.67; J. Hassell, *Picturesque Rides and Walks* (London, 1817-18), i.96; D.C. Whimster, *The Archaeology of Surrey* (London, 1931), pp.7-8, 138. No location has been established: the most recent suggestion is Great Woodcote Farm at Farm Lane, Purley: Muckelroy, *art. cit.*, p.42; also 'Medieval Woodcote,' *Local History Records*, xiii (Bourne Society, 1974), pp.6-9.

68 Powell, *Court Rolls*, p.33 (which corrects the statement in Muckelroy, *art. cit.*, p.41). Kechyn or Kychyn was still a Beddington surname in 1545/46: see below, pp.69, 74.

69 Phillipps Collection MSS (Surrey Record Office): Thomas Mabson's accounts for February-May 1550.

70 *VCH*, iv.170.

From Woodcote a road ran down to Beddington. It may have formed the western boundary of Bandon: it was certainly the eastern edge of the South Field of Beddington.[71] This being so, it is not entirely clear why a Bandon court should have been required to take note of an issue concerning land west of the road although it may have simply been the case that by 1545 memories of the boundary between Bandon and Beddington were becoming hazy and there was no desire to make a strict separation of business between them. Yet the Bandon court record for that year contains important evidence for elucidating what was meant by lands pertaining to the Beddington Portion. As mentioned above, Mr. K.A. Pryer has shown[72] that the portioner was a lay-presented cleric, originally distinct from the rector of Beddington and probably attached to Merton Priory, who seems to have been endowed with a royal grant of land and tithes in 1215. The tithes were levied on 200 acres (including a mansion and a watermill) of Huscarls land, which lay north of the Wandle: but the portioner had a house and an area of land which were both south of the river. According to testimony presented at the Chancery hearing of 1472, the portioner's house and land, stated to be twenty acres in extent, were also to the south side of the church.

[71] Below, p.65; cf. Michell, *Carews*, p.12, who suggests that this road followed the line of the modern Demesne Road, but follows Pryer (see next note), pp.3 41, 49, in locating the actual boundary between the manors slightly to the east at Queen Elizabeth's Walk continuing southwards to connect with Sandy Lane. I suspect that this road was the Green Street or Greenw of the 1514 survey rather than Sandy Lane: see Pryer pp.40-2.

[72] See above, p.xxiv; and Pryer, *Beddington Portion*, pp.14, 25-4.

> Says he knows not when or in what manner it began and being interrogated in what part of the Parish aforesaid the said Portion exists says there is a certain Mansion with 20 acres of land belonging to the said Portion and the Portionary, which are situate on the south part of the Church aforesaid and on the north part of the said Church there are situate 200 acres of land vulgarly called Huscarls Fee, of which 200 acres of land the Portionary takes and has the Tythes arising therefrom and said the said Portion is donative but whether it is taxed or valued he knows not.[73]

Threequarters of a century later, in 1545, the members of the Bandon homage are to be found swearing[74] that at the beginning of the sixteenth century there had been some eleven acres of portionary land which had since been enclosed into Beddington Park: eight acres of 'porcionaryffeld' and an adjoining three acres which had now come to form the Carews' 'New Orchard' - which would again seem to imply proximity to Carew Manor itself. This enclosure took place between 1514 and 1520, when Sir Richard Carew was lord of the manor, and the portioner was the rector of Beddington himself, which no doubt facilitated the matter. In exchange the rector, as portioner, received fourteen acres in the South Field west of the road to Woodcote. This did not however prevent his successor thirty years later from being faced with a claim by the royal administrators of

[73] Cited Pryer, *Beddington Portion*, p.22. Michell, *Carews*, p.12, also follows Pryer, pp.26 and 42-3, in putting the Portioner's house on the south-west side of the Church near the junction of Church Road and Croydon Road.

[74] Below, pp.65-6.

Beddington that this land in the South Field ought to be reclaimed for the manor - until the sworn testimony of local inhabitants at the court of 1545 served to prove otherwise.

Whereas the Bandon manor material provides a rich quarry for local historians, the handful of Beddington court records have relatively little to offer. The main reason for this is that the Bandon entries, as fa as one can judge these matters, do indeed relate to th area covered by the manor of Bandon.[75] But the Carew seem on the other hand to have used the Beddington court, at least on some occasions, as a central court for several of their numerous Surrey lands and estates and a high proportion of the material in the Beddingtc record is not for Beddington itself. This is not immediately apparent. The first surviving record, for the court held in January 1519, contains personal and place-names (Sir Lawrence Gylemer, John Bristowe o Logge, the Pope and Skinner families, Strode Field by 'Bentyngwode', or New Field) which would be sure to tantalise a Beddington historian eager to identify them, did we not also have the March 1528 court record to compare it with. This shows that the earlier cour had apparently dealt with no Beddington business at al since most of the names listed in 1519 relate to Horle and Reigate.[76] Only the reference to the Pope family

[75] Which does not of course prevent Bandon inhabitants from having Beddington connections. Thus three generations of the Legger family had a house and twenty-six acres in Beddington (below, p.71); and in 1545-6 William Legger acted as the constable of Beddington (p.69), but paid homage at the Bandon court (e.g. p.65) and his death was recorded there (p.71). In 1545 John and Joan Ridley had a house and garden in Beddington, previously belonging to Helen Skete, which Joan obtained through her first husband John Dabourne which was all dealt with at Bandon sessions (pp.66, 71

[76] The inclusion of Horley as early as 1519 is

who came from Woodhatch in Reigate, and to the prior of the house of Augustinian Canons at Reigate (dissolved in 1536), provide clues to the fact that these were not Carew tenants at Beddington itself. Later Beddington courts clearly combined business both from Beddington and from other manors: besides Reigate and Horley, Chessington - which appears to have been very foreign to the scribe, since it appears in various forms as Chysynden, Rysyndon, even Chesruden[77] - is also dealt with at Beddington, and it is particularly interesting that in 1546 the Beddington jury were requiring Chessington tenants who had land 'between Parson's Acre and Pinner's Close' to clean out their ditches by an appointed day in September.[78] If a complete run of Beddington manor court rolls is ever recovered, it will be a major undertaking to sort out the properties involved, and we can perhaps feel more relieved than disappointed at the scanty information on offer about Beddington. Apart from the names of some of the inhabitants, and the usual complaints that millers and innkeepers were giving short measure,[79] we can

interesting, since it is generally held that Horley came to Sir Nicholas Carew in 1538 after the dissolution of Chertsey Abbey: Michell, *Carews*, p.40. Some Chertsey land at Horley had always owed suit of court to the manor of Sutton: *Chertsey Abbey Cartularies*, ii.l. p.284.

[77] Below, pp.68 and 73-5: William Brokhole, tithing man of 'Rysyndon' and 'Chesruden', was elected constable of Chessington in 1546.

[78] Below, p.74.

[79] Below pp.68-9, 74. The Henry Gaynysford who is convicted of both offences in 1545 must be the Henry Gainsford of Carshalton, 'common brewer and miller', who was also possessor of the manor of Stone Court and its mills, but had alienated a moiety of the estate to Sir Roger and Elizabeth Copley the previous year: see above, p.xi at n.11; and Powell, *Court Rolls*, p.viii. He made his will in 1545 and died in the early months of the following year.

learn little about the physical character of Beddingt in the sixteenth century. The courts between 1545 a 1549 were held whilst Beddington was in the hands of the crown after the execution of Sir Nicholas Carew i 1539, and the royal administrators (apart from confiscating the odd stray horse[80]) were really only interested in seeing that the king's highways were ke up and improved. In 1545 the inhabitants were set t work digging a new road called 'Pyttlent',[81] after which their shovels seem to have been in need of repair;[82] and the following year Nicholas Broke was fined for allowing the branches of his tree to grow over the road 'toward Surrey's land'.[83] But in general there was little to do: and the last of our Beddington courts held on 23 April 1549 provides an apt epilogue to the proceedings - 'No one appeared at the court, because they were not warned of it.'[84]

[80] Below, pp.69-70.

[81] Below, p.69.

[82] Below, p.74.

[83] Below, pp.74-5.

[84] Below, p.77.

M.J.W.

Cur*ie* Maner*ii* de

Bandon de 13° H*enrici* 7

vsq*ue* ad 22 H*enrici* 8 &

3 & 6 E*dwardi* 6

Bedyngton

[10° &] 19° H*enrici* 8

Courts of the Manor of

Bandon from 13th Henry VII (1498)

to 22nd Henry VIII (1531) and

3rd and 6th Edward VI (1549 and 1552)

Beddington

[10th and] 19th Henry VIII (1519 and 1528)

with the addition of 36th, 37th and 38th

Henry VIII (1545 and 1546)

from the Public Record Office

Bandon — Cur*ia* Ric*ard*i Carewe milit*is* ib*id*em tent*a* xij^{mo} die mensis Marcij Anno R*egni* R*egis* Henrici vij^{ti} xiij^{mo}

Essoni*um* — Null*um*

fidel*itas* — Ad istam ven*it* Joh*ann*es Chantrell p*ro* se & cofeoffat*is* suis ad vsum Ric*ard*i Botteler & hered*um* suo*rum* & cognou*it* Se tenere libere p*er* carta*m* vnu*m* ten*ementum* [ ] p*er* fidel*itatem* & Reddit*um* iij^{s}j^{d} ob*oli* p*er* Annu*m* Sect*am* Cur*ie* h*er*iett*um* & Rel*evium* cu*m* acciderit Et fecit d*omi*no fidel*itatem*

fidel*itas* — Ad istam ven*it* Nich*ol*aus Waker & cogn*ovit* Se tenere de d*omi*no libere p*er* carta*m* vnu*m* ten*ementum* & Centu*m* Acras te*r*re cu*m* suis p*er*tin*enciis* quond*am* vocat*a* Gargett*es*[1] p*er* fidel*itatem* & reddit*um* vj^{s}vij^{d} p*er* an*num* Sect*am* Cur*ie* h*er*iett*um* & Rel*evium* cu*m* acciderit Et fecit d*omi*no fidel*itatem*

fidel*itas* — Ad istam ven*it* Joh*ann*es payn & cogn*ovit* Se tenere libere p*er* carta*m* vnu*m* ten*ementum* cum gardino adiacent*i* cu*m* suis p*er*t*inenciis* nup*er* Wakers p*er* fidel*itatem* & reddit*um* XX^{d} p*er* an*num* Sect*am* Cur*ie* h*er*iett*um* & Rel*evium* cu*m* accide*r*it Et fec*it* d*omi*no fidel*itatem*

fidel*itas* — Ad istam ven*it* Ric*ard*us Adam & cogn*ovit* Se tenere lib*ere* p*er* cart*am* vnu*m* ten*ementum* cum

[1] Erasure.

Bandon

A court of Richard Carewe, knight, held there on the twelfth day of the month of March in the thirteenth year of the reign of King Henry VII. 1498

Essoin

None

Fealty

To this *court* came John Chantrell for himself and his fellows, feoffed to the use of Richard Botteler and his heirs, and acknowledged that he holds freely by charter a tenement [ ] for fealty and a rent of $3^{s}1\frac{1}{2}^{d}$ a year, suit at court, heriot, and relief when it falls due. And he did fealty to the lord.

Fealty

To this *court* came Nicholas Waker and acknowledged that he holds of the lord, freely by charter, a tenement and a hundred acres of land with their appurtenances, formerly called Gargettes, [1] for fealty and a rent of $6^{s}7^{d}$ a year, suit at court, heriot, and relief when it falls due. And he did fealty to the lord.

Fealty

To this *court* came John Payn and acknowledged that he holds freely by charter a tenement with a garden adjacent with their appurtenances, formerly Waker's, for fealty and a rent of 20^{d} a year, suit at court, heriot, and relief when it falls due. And he did fealty to the lord.

Fealty

To this *court* came Richard Adam and acknowledged that he holds freely by charter a tenement with

gardino & quinque Acr*as* terre cu*m* suis per*tinenciis* nup*er* Norfolk*is* p*er* fidel*itatem* & reddit*um* xviij^{d} p*er* an*num* Sect*am* Cur*ie* her*iett*um* & Rel*evium* cu*m* accid*er*it Et fecit d*omi*no fidel*itatem*

fidel*itas* Ad istam ven*it* Will*elmus* Ligeard & cogn*ovit* Se ten*er*e de d*omi*no libere p*er* carta*m* vnu*m* ten*ementum* cu*m* gardino & viginti sex acr*as* t*er*re cu*m* suis p*er*tin*enciis* nup*er* Whelers p*er* fidel*itatem* & reddit*um* xxij^{d} p*er* an*num* Sect*am* Cur*ie* h*er*iett*um* & Rel*evium* cu*m* accid*er*it Et fecit d*omi*no fidel*itatem*

fidel*itas* Ad istam ven*it* Joh*annes* Waker & cogn*ovit* Se tenere libere p*er* carta*m* vnu*m* toftu*m* & di*midiam* acr*am* t*er*re Arabil*is* quond*am* Mokyls p*er* fidel*itatem* & reddit*um* xx^{d} p*er* an*num* Sect*am* Cur*ie* h*er*iett*um* & Rel*evium* cu*m* accid*er*it Et fec*it* d*omi*no fidel*itatem*

homagi*um* Joh*annes* Chantrell Joh*annes* payn Will*elmus* Legyard Nich*ol*aus Waker Ric*ar*dus Adam Joh*annes* Waker Jur*ati*

m*isericordia* xviij^{d} Qui dic*unt* sup*er* Sacr*amentu*m suu*m* q*uo*d Robert*us* Morley (ij^{d}) in Jure vx*or*is sue nup*er* vx*or*is Will*elm*i Cleybrok Will*elmus* Mychell Civis & dyer london (ij^{d}) p*ro* t*er*ris quond*am* Joh*annis* Ball Joh*annes* Botery (ij^{d}) p*ro* t*er*ris quond*am* ffauxwellys Nich*ol*aus Burton de ffulham (ij^{d}) p*ro* t*er*ris quond*am* Russell Nich*ol*aus Glover (ij^{d}) Joh*annes* Waker (ij^{d}) Joh*annes* Batyson (ij^{d}) p*ro* t*er*ris quond*am* Norfolk*is* Joh*annes* haccher Colyer (ij^{d}) dionis*ia* Neuport de london

a garden and five acres of land with their appurtenances, formerly Norfolk's, for fealty and a rent of 18^d a year, suit at court, heriot, and relief when it falls due. And he did fealty to the lord. 1498

Fealty

To this *court* came William Ligeard and acknowledged that he holds of the lord, freely by charter, a tenement with a garden and twenty-six acres of land with their appurtenances, formerly Wheler's, for fealty and a rent of 22^d a year, suit at court, heriot, and relief when it falls due. And he did fealty to the lord.

Fealty

To this *court* came John Waker and acknowledged that he holds freely by charter a toft and half an acre of arable land, formerly Mokyl's, for fealty and a rent of 20^d a year, suit at court, heriot, and relief when it falls due. And he did fealty to the lord.

Homage

John Chantrell	John Payn	William Legyard
Nicholas Waker	Richard Adam	John Waker
		Sworn

Amercement 18^d

These say upon their oath that Robert Morley (2^d) in right of his wife, formerly the wife of William Cleybrok; William Mychell, alderman and dyer of London (2^d), for lands formerly John Ball's; John Botery (2^d), for lands formerly Fauxwell's; Nicholas Burton of Fulham (2^d), for lands formerly Russell's; Nicholas Glover (2^d); John Waker (2^d); John Batyson (2^d), for lands formerly Norfolk's; John Haccher, collier (2^d), Dionisia Neuport of London, widow vidua (ij^{d}) p*ro* t*er*ris quond*am* Camberwyll*is* Tenen*s* t*err*e nup*er* Saunder (in m*isericordia* d*omi*ni) Elizabeth Boteler vidua (ij^{d}) p*ro* t*erris* quond*am* holden Et p*ro* Resid*entarii* veredict*o* sui dicend*o* petunt diem hic vs*que* p*r*ox*imam* Cur*iam* & eis concedit*ur*

Su*m*ma huiu*s* Cur*ie* xviij^{d}

(2^d), for lands formerly Camberwyll's; the 1498
tenant of land formerly Saunder's (in mercy of the lord); Elizabeth Boteler, widow (2^d), for lands formerly Holden's, seek a day between now and the next court for a verdict to be announced on their residentiary claims and it is conceded to them.

Amount of this court 18^d

Bandon — Cur*i*a Ric*ard*i Carewe milit*is* ib*i*d*e*m tent*a* die Marcurij p*roxi*m*o* ante f*est*u*m* Nat*ivitatis* be*ate* Marie A*nn*o R*egni* R*egis* henrici vij^{ti} xv^{mo}

Essoni*um* — Null*um*

homagiu*m* — Nich*ol*aus Waker   Wille*lmus* legeard   Joh*ann*es payn   Joh*ann*es Waker   Jur*ati*

m*isericordia* xx^{d} — Qui dic*unt* sup*er* Sacr*amentum* suu*m* q*uo*d Robert*us* Morley (ij^{d}) in Jure vx*or*is sue Wille*lmus* Michell Civis & dyer london (ij^{d}) Joh*ann*es Botery (ij^{d}) Nich*ol*aus Burton de ffulh*a*m (ij^{d}) Nich*ol*aus Glouer (ij^{d}) Joh*ann*es Batyson (ij^{d}) Joh*ann*es haccher Colyer (ij^{d}) dionis*i*a Neuport de london vidua (ij^{d}) Ten*ens* te*r*rar*um* nup*er* Saunder (in m*isericordia* dom*i*ni) Elizabeth Boteler vidua (ij^{d}) Joh*ann*es Chantrell (ij^{d}) p*ro* se & cofeoffatis suis ad vsu*m* Ric*ard*i Boteler & hered*um* suo*rum* deb*ent* Sect*am* Cur*i*e & fecer*unt* defalt*am* J*de*o ip*s*i & *cetera*

Obit*us* — Jtem dic*unt* q*uo*d henric*us* hunt qui de dom*i*no tenuit libere quin*que* Acras te*r*re in Bandon p*er* fidel*itatem* & Reddit*um* x^{d} p*er* an*num* obijt cit*ra* vlt*imam* Cur*iam* post cuius mort*em* accid*it* dom*i*no de he*r*iett*o* vn*us* bos p*re*cij vij^{s} Et dic*unt* vlteri*us* q*uo*d Thom*as* hunt p*re*sens in Cur*i*a est filius eius & heres & plene etat*is* & p*ro*fert cartam Cur*i*e cui*us* dat*a* est xx^{mo} die mensis Aprilis A*nn*o xiiij^{o} R*egis* henrici septimi p*er* qua*m* apparet q*uo*d idem Thom*as* inde feoffauit

he*r*iett*um* j bos p*re*cii vij^{s}

Bandon — A court of Richard Carewe, knight, held there on the Wednesday next before the feast of the Nativity of the blessed Mary (4th September) in the fifteenth year of the reign of King Henry VII. 1499

Essoin — None

Homage — Nicholas Waker, William Legeard, John Payn, John Waker — Sworn

Amercement — These say upon their oath that Robert Morley (2^d) in right of his wife; William Michell, alderman and dyer of London (2^d); John Botery (2^d); Nicholas Burton of Fulham (2^d); Nicholas Glover (2^d); John Batyson (2^d); John Haccher, collier (2^d); Dionisia Neuport of London, widow (2^d); the tenant of lands formerly Saunder's (in mercy of the lord); Elizabeth Boteler, widow (2^d); John Chantrell (2^d) for himself and his fellows feoffed to the use of Richard Boteler and his heirs, owe suit at court and have made default. Therefore, they etc..

Death

Heriot: one ox worth 7^s

Also, they say that Henry Hunt, who held freely of the lord five acres of land in Bandon for fealty and a rent of 10^d a year, has died since the last court, after whose death there fell to the lord as heriot an ox worth 7^s. And they further say that Thomas Hunt, present in court, is his son and heir and of full age and presents to the court a charter, the date of which is the 20th day of the month of April in the fourteenth year of King Henry VII (1499), by which it appears

Joh*ann*em Waker Joh*ann*em Carpent*er* & Nich*ol*aum
Crystmas in feodo in dict*is* quin*que* acris
p*er* nome*n* om*ni*um t*er*ra*rum* & ten*ementorum*
suo*rum* in villa & campis de Bedyngton
Walyngton & carsalton in Com*itatu* Surr*ey*
quiquide*m* Joh*ann*es Waker p*re*sens in Cur*ia*
fidel*itas* — fec*it* d*omi*no fidel*itatem* p*ro* se & sociis
suis Et vlteri*us* pr*eceptum* e*st* b*alli*o
dis*tringere* — dis*tringere* t*er*ra*s* & ten*ementa* p*re*dicta
p*ro* Rel*evio* — p*ro* Rel*evio* post mort*em* p*re*d*i*ct*i* henrici
erga p*r*ox*imam* Cur*iam*

S*um*m*a* hui*us* Cur*ie* viij^{s}viij^{d}

that the same Thomas therein feoffed John 1499
Waker, John Carpenter and Nicholas Crystmas
in fee in the said five acres by name of all
his lands and tenements in the vill and fields
of Beddington, Wallington and Carshalton in the
County of Surrey. The same John Waker,
Fealty present in court, did fealty to the lord for
himself and his fellows. And further, the
Distrain order is given to the bailiff to distrain the
for relief lands and tenements aforementioned for relief
after the death of the aforesaid Henry by the
next court.

Amount of this court $8^s 8^d$

Bandon — Cur*ia* Ric*ard*i Carewe milit*is* ib*ide*m tent*a* xiij^{mo} die mensis Octobris A*nno* R*e*g*ni* R*e*g*is* henrici septimi xvj^{mo}

Essoni*um* — Null*um*

homagi*um* — Joh*anne*s Botery Ville*lmus* legger Joh*anne*s Waker
Nich*ola*us Waker Joh*anne*s haccher
Thom*a*s hunt Thom*a*s lewys

Jur*ati*

m*isericordia* xx^{d} — Qui dic*unt* sup*er* Sacr*amentu*m suu*m* q*uo*d Robert*us* Morley (ij^{d}) Joh*anne*s Payne (ij^{d}) Nich*ola*us Burton de ffulh*a*m (ij^{d}) Nich*ola*us Glouer (ij^{d}) Wille*lmus* Aleyn fili*us* Thome Aleyn (ij^{d}) Wille*lmus* lee (ij^{d}) in Jure katerine vx*or*is sue Wille*lmus* Batyson (ij^{d}) dionisia Neuport vidua (ij^{d}) Elizabeth Boteler (ij^{d}) Cristofer*us* litton Rector de Bedyngton (ij^{d}) deb*ent* Sect*am* Cur*ie* & fec*erunt* defalt*am* J*deo* & cetera

Obit*us* — Comp*er*tu*m* est p*er* homagiu*m* q*uo*d Wille*lmus* Michell qui de d*omi*no tenuit libere vnu*m* ten*ementum* ac div*ersa*s te*r*ras & ten*ementa* in Bandon nup*er* Joh*anni*s Ball & quond*a*m poyntes & p*re*antea Reysons per fidel*itatem* & reddit*um* xix^{d} p*er* an*num* Sect*am* Cur*ie* & alia se*r*uicia obijt cit*ra* ult*imam* Cur*iam* post cui*us* morte*m* pr*eceptum* est ball*io* seisire optimu*m* an*i*m*a*ll ipsi*us* Wille*lmi* p*ro* he*r*iett*o* Et dic*unt* vlteri*us* quod [ ] que*m* pr*eceptum* est ball*io* dis*tringere* p*ro* Rel*evio* & fidel*itate* erga p*roxi*m*am* Cur*iam*

dis*tringere* p*ro* he*r*iett*o* & xix^{d} de Rel*evio*

Bandon

A court of Richard Carewe, knight, held there on the thirteenth day of the month of October in the sixteenth year of the reign of King Henry VII. 1500

Essoin

None

Homage

John Botery	William Legger	John Waker
Nicholas Waker	John Haccher	
Thomas Hunt	Thomas Lewys	

Sworn

Amercement 20^d

These say upon their oath that Robert Morley (2^d); John Payne (2^d); Nicholas Burton of Fulham (2^d); Nicholas Glover (2^d); William Aleyn, son of Thomas Aleyn (2^d); William Lee (2^d) in right of Katherine his wife; William Batyson (2^d); Dionisia Neuport, widow (2^d); Elizabeth Boteler (2^d); Christopher Litton, rector of Beddington (2^d), owe suit at court and have made default. Therefore etc..

Death

It is found by the homage that William Michell, who held freely of the lord a tenement and various lands and tenements in Bandon, late of John Ball and before that Poynte's and earlier Reyson's, for fealty and a rent of 19^d a year, suit at court and other services, has died since the last court, after whose death the order is given to the bailiff to seize the best beast of the same William as heriot. And they say further that [ ] the order is given to the bailiff to distrain him for relief and fealty before the next court.

Distrain for heriot and 19^d of relief

Alienac*io* — Jt*em* dic*unt* q*uo*d Nich*ola*us Waker qui de
d*om*ino tenuit libere vnu*m* ten*ementum* ac
diu*ersas* te*rras* p*er* fidel*itatem* & Redditu*m*
pr*o*ut p*atet* in Rent*a*li Alias feoffauit
pa*r*ce*lla* ten*ementi* — Joh*ann*em Barett in xxx Acr*is* te*r*re pa*r*cell*a*
dict*i* ten*ementi* in feodo mo*do* Roberti Morley
Et petit reddit*um* te*r*re p*r*edict*e* Apporcionari
Et hoc non obstante p*receptum* e*st* ball*io*
dis*tringere* dict*um* [ ] [1]
p*ro* integro redditu quousq*ue* apporcionat*um*
se*cun*d*um* forma*m* Statuti inde edit*i*

Alienac*io* — Jt*e*m dic*unt* q*uo*d Ric*ard*us Adam qui de d*omi*no
tenuit vnu*m* ten*ementum* [et] quinq*ue* acr*as*
& di*midiam* p*er* fidel*itatem* & reddit*um* xviij^{d}
sect*am* Cur*ie* & alia s*er*uicia inde feoffauit
Joh*ann*em Botery in feodo quiquid*e*m Joh*ann*es
fidel*itas* — p*r*esens in Cur*i*a fec*it* d*omi*no fidel*itatem*

dis*tringere* — Pr*eceptum* est ball*io* dis*tringere* Robertu*m*
Morley p*ro* iij^{s}iiij^{d} p*er* ips*um* subtract*a*
p*ro* te*r*ris voc*atis* Dogg*e*s nup*er* Thom*e* Warh*a*m
pr*o*ut p*atet* p*er* Rentall Joh*ann*is Chantrell

dis*tringere* — Pre*ceptum* est ball*io* dis*tringere* Wille*lm*um
legeard p*ro* iiij^{d} de Reddit*u* p*er* ips*um* subtract*o*

Ad istam ven*it* Joh*ann*es Botery in Jure Johanne
vx*o*ris sue filie Joh*ann*is ffawxwell & fec*it*
fidel*itas* — d*omi*no fidel*itatem* p*ro* te*r*ris nup*er* dicti
Joh*ann*is & quond*a*m lucas   Necnon p*ro* vno

[1] Erasure.

1500

Alienation

Also, they say that Nicholas Waker, who held freely of the lord a tenement and various lands for fealty and a rent as appears in a rental elsewhere, feoffed John Barett in thirty

Parcel of tenement

acres of land, a parcel of the said tenement in fee now of Robert Morley. And he seeks that the rent of the aforementioned land be apportioned. And, notwithstanding this, the order is given to the bailiff to distrain the said [ ] [1] for the whole rent until it shall have been apportioned, according to the form of the Statute therefor enacted.

Alienation

Also, they say that Richard Adam who held of the lord a tenement [and] five and a half acres for fealty and a rent of 18^{d}, suit at court and other services, therein feoffed John Botery in fee, and the same John, present

Fealty

in court, did fealty to the lord.

Distrain

The order is given to the bailiff to distrain Robert Morley for $3^{s}4^{d}$ witheld by him for lands called Dogges, formerly of Thomas Warham, as appears on the rental of John Chantrell.

Distrain

The order is given to the bailiff to distrain William Legeard for 4^{d} rent witheld by him.

To this *court* came John Botery in right of Joan his wife, daughter of John Fawxwell, and did

Fealty

fealty to the lord for lands late of the said John and formerly of Lucas, and also for a gardino sup*er* l*e* Sandhyll quond*am* d*i*cti lucas & antea Bygott*is*

Jdem Joh*anne*s Botery in Jure suo p*r*op*ri*o fec*it* d*omi*no fidel*itatem* p*ro* t*er*ris nup*er* Adams

S*umma* hui*us* Cur*ie* iij^{s}iij^{d}

garden on le Sandhill, late of the said Lucas and before that Bygott's. 1500

The same John Botery in his own right did fealty to the lord for lands formerly Adam's.

Amount of this court $3^s 3^d$

Bandon	Cur*ia* Ric*ardi* Carew Milit*is* ib*idem* tent*a* die Martis *proximo* post fe*stum* s*ancti* Georgij m*artyri*s anno Re*gni* Re*gis* henrici septimi xvj^{o}
Essoni*um*	Null*um*
homagi*um*	Joh*annes* Botery — Thomas hunt Nich*ol*aus Waker — Thomas lews Will*elmus* legeard

Jur*ati*

m*isericordia* xviij^{d}	Qui dic*unt* sup*er* Sacr*amentum* suu*m* q*uod* Robert Morley (ij^{d}) Nich*ol*aus Burton de ffulh*a*m (ij^{d}) Nich*ol*aus Glouer (ij^{d}) ⌈ ⌉ [1] heredes Thome holden (ij^{d}) Will*elmus* le (ij^{d}) dionisia Newport (ij^{d}) Will*elmus* Batyson (ij^{d}) & Joh*annes* haccher (ij^{d}) deb*ent* Sect*am* ⌈Cur*ie* & fec*erunt*⌉ defalt*am* J*deo* ip*si* separ*atim* in m*isericordia* & c*etera*
Obit*us* Rel*evium* xx sol*utum* d*omino* in duob*us* ouib*us* dis*tringere* p*ro* fidel*itate*	Comp*er*tum es*t* p*er* homagiu*m* q*uo*d Joh*annes* payn qui de d*omi*no tenuit libere vnu*m* ten*ementum* cum gardino adjacent*i* nup*er* Wakers & quondam Cutbyes per fidel*itatem* & reddit*um* xx^{d} p*er* an*num* Sect*am* Cur*ie* h*er*iett*um* & Rel*evium* cum acciderit obijt cit*ra* vlt*imam* Cur*iam* post cui*us* mortem accid*it* d*omi*no de h*er*iett*o* vnus aries p*re*cij xvj^{d} deliberat*us* ad ⌈stab*ulum*⌉ d*omi*ni per Nich*olaum* ⌈Gamidg⌉ Et vlterius dic*unt* q*uo*d Joh*annes* payn est eius filius & heres p*ro*pinquior & est etat*is* tresdecem annorum & amplius quem pre*ceptum* est ball*io* dis*tringere* p*ro* fidel*itate* erga p*roximam* Cur*iam*

[1] A piece of the manuscript is missing.

andon A court of Richard Carew, knight, held there on the Tuesday next after the feast of Saint George the Martyr (27th April) in the sixteenth year of the reign of King Henry VII. 1501

ssoin None

omage

John Botery Thomas Hunt
Nicholas Waker Thomas Lews
William Legeard

Sworn

mercement 18^{d}

These say upon their oath that Robert Morley (2^{d}), Nicholas Burton of Fulham (2^{d}), Nicholas Glover (2^{d}), [ ] [1] the heirs of Thomas Holden (2^{d}), William Lee (2^{d}), Dionisia Newport (2^{d}), William Batyson (2^{d}) and John Haccher (2^{d}) owe suit [at court and have made] default. Therefore they are severally in mercy etc..

eath

It is found by the homage that John Payn, who held freely of the lord a tenement with garden adjacent, late Waker's and formerly Cutbye's, for fealty and a rent of 20^{d} a year, suit at court, heriot, and relief when it falls due, has died since the last court, after whose death there fell to the lord as heriot a ram worth 16^{d} which was delivered to the lord's [barn] by Nicholas [Gamidg]. And they further say that John Payn is his son and nearest heir and is thirteen years of age and more. The order is given to the bailiff to distrain him for fealty before the next court.

elief 20^{d}
aid to the
ord in the
orm of two
heep
istrain
or fealty

Obit*us*	Jt*em* dic*unt* q*uo*d Will*elmus* Aleyn qui de d*omi*no tenuit libere vnu*m* ten*ementum* nup*er* Thome Aleyn & quond*a*m allott*is* p*er* fidel*itatem* & reddit*um* xij^{d} p*er* an*num* Sect*am* Cur*ie* h*er*iett*um* & Rel*evium* cu*m* acciderit obijt cit*ra* vlt*imam* Cur*iam* post cui*us* morte*m* n*ihi*l accid*it* d*omi*no de h*er*iett*o* q*uia* null*um* h*ab*uit a*n*im*a*ll Et vlterius dic*unt* q*uo*d lucia Aleyn est eius soror & heres p*ro*pinquior & plene etat*is* qua*m* pr*eceptum* est ball*io* dist*ringere* p*ro* fidel*itate* & Rel*evio* erga p*ro*x*imam* Cur*iam*
dis*tringere* p*ro* fidel*itate* & xij^{d} de Rel*evio*	
Obit*us*	Jt*em* dic*unt* q*uo*d Dionisia Newport que de d*omi*no tenuit libere duas acras nup*er* Johanne Cooke filie & heres Ric*ardi* Camberwell p*er* fidel*itatem* & reddit*um* viij^{d} p*er* an*num* Sect*am* Cur*ie* h*er*iett*um* & Rel*evium* cu*m* acciderit obijt cit*ra* vlt*imam* Cur*iam* post cui*us* morte*m* n*ihi*l accid*it* d*omi*no de h*er*iett*o* q*uia* null*um* h*ab*uit a*n*im*a*ll
pr*eceptum*	Pr*eceptum* est alicie vincent Margarete hwe Margarete haccher katerine Makyns alicie [ ] [1] alicie Jsak q*uo*d ips*e* [2] decetero non frangant cepes nec portant aliqua ligna a wode [ ] [3] sub pe*na* xij^{d}
pr*eceptum*	Pr*eceptum* est cuili*be*t tenenci*um* infra man*er*ium ib*ide*m habent*ium* porcos tam eos

[1] A piece of the manuscript is missing.

[2] MS: ip*s*i

[3] A piece of the manuscript is missing.

)eath

Also, they say that William Aleyn, who held freely of the lord a tenement, late of Thomas Aleyn and formerly Allott's, for fealty and a rent of 12^{d} a year, suit at court, heriot, and relief when it falls due, has died since the last court, after whose death nothing fell to the lord as heriot because he had no beast. And further, they say that Lucy Aleyn is his sister and nearest heir and of full age. The order is given to the bailiff to distrain her for fealty and relief before the next court. 1501

)istrain for :ealty and .2^{d} for ·elief

Death

Also, they say that Dionisia Newport, who held freely of the lord two acres formerly of Joan Cooke, daughter and heir of Richard Camberwell, for fealty and a rent of 8^{d} a year, suit at court, heriot and relief when it falls due, has died since the last court. After her death nothing fell to the lord as heriot because she had no beast.

Order

The order is given to Alice Vincent, Margaret Hwe, Margaret Haccher, Katherine Makyns, Alice [ ], [1] Alice Jsak, that they [2] do not henceforth break down the hedges or carry away any firewood from Wode [ ] [3] under penalty of 12^{d}.

Order

The order is given to each and every tenant within the manor who has pigs therein both to

anulare qu*am* [eos justificare cit*ra* f*estu*m Nativitatis] d*omi*ni p*ro*x*imum* futu*rum* sub pe*na* cuiusl*ibe*t eo*rum* xij^{d}

m*isericordia* iij^{s} Jt*em* dic*unt* q*uo*d Joh*ann*es Bereman (xij^{d}) Brown vanryggon (xij^{d}) petrus Bereman (xij^{d}) indies transiunt [sine] licencia d*omi*ni [et tenenc*ium*] man*er*ij ib*id*em cu*m* carect*is* suis J*d*eo ip*s*i sep*ar*atim in m*isericord*ia p*ro*ut p*atet* sup*er* eo*rum* Capit*a* vel versus eos fiat accio

S*um*ma huiu*s* Cur*ie* iiij^{s}vj^{d}

ring them and [to license them] before 1501
the feast of the Nativity of the Lord next
to come under penalty, for each and every
one of them, of 12^{d}.

mercement 3^{s}

Also, they say that John Bereman (12^{d}),
Brown Vanryggon (12^{d}), Peter Bereman (12^{d}),
daily cross there [without] the permission
of the lord [and tenants] of the manor
with their carts. Therefore they are
severally in mercy as appears above their
heads, or let an action be brought against
them.

Amount of this court $4^{s}6^{d}$

Bandon

Cur*ia* ib*ide*m tent*a* decimo tercio die Maij Anno r*egni* r*egis* henrici septimi decimo septimo

Essoni*um*

Nul*lum*

Homagi*um*

Will*elmu*s Bateson Will*elmu*s legeard Thom*a*s lews Nich*ol*aus Waker Nich*ol*aus Glouer sen*ior* Joh*anne*s Waker sen*ior* Thom*a*s huntt

Jur*ati*

m*isericordia* xviij^{d}

Qui dic*unt* sup*er* Sacr*amentu*m suu*m* q*uo*d Robert*us* Morley (ij^{d}) Nich*ol*aus Burton de ffulham (ij^{d}) hered*es* Thome holden (ij^{d}) Will*elmu*s lee (ij^{d}) Dionis*ia* Newport (ij^{d}) Joh*anne*s hacch*er* (ij^{d}) Joh*anne*s Botrye (ij^{d}) Joh*anne*s payn (ij^{d}) & lucia Aleyn (ij^{d}) deb*ent* Sect*am* Cur*ie* & fec*erunt* defalt*am* J*de*o ip*s*i in m*isericordia*

ffin*is* Sect*e* Cur*ie* vj^{d}

Ad istam ven*it* Will*elmu*s Bateson (vj^{d}) & Dat d*omi*no de ffin*e* p*ro* Sect*a* Cur*ie* Rela*xata* hoc anno p*ro*ut p*ate*t in Capite

dies

Dies dat*us* est Tenent*ibus* ib*ide*m ad habend*um* vnu*m* pastorem ad Custod*ienda* an*i*malia sua citr*a* f*es*tum Corp*or*is *Christ*i sub pen*a* vj^{s}viij^{d}

pr*eceptum*

Pr*eceptum* est q*uo*d null*i* Tenenciu*m* ib*ide*m decetero Custod*iant* aliquod ouile nisi illi qui ex antiquo h*ab*uerunt citr*a* f*es*tu*m* Mich*ae*lis quia sunt ib*ide*m nisi tria vt dic*unt* sub pen*a* x^{s}

andon

A court held there on the thirteenth day of May in the seventeenth year of the reign of King Henry VII. 1502

ssoin

None

omage

William Bateson	William Legeard	Thomas Lews
Nicholas Waker	Nicholas Glover senior	
John Waker senior	Thomas Huntt	

Sworn

nercement 18^{d}

These say upon their oath that Robert Morley (2^{d}), Nicholas Burton of Fulham (2^{d}), the heirs of Thomas Holden (2^{d}), William Lee (2^{d}), Dionisia Newport (2^{d}), John Haccher (2^{d}), John Botrye (2^{d}), John Payn (2^{d}) and Lucy Aleyn (2^{d}) owe suit at court and have made default. Therefore they are in mercy.

ine of suit t court 6^{d}

To this *court* comes William Bateson(6^{d}) and gives to the lord as a fine for suit at court, remitted this year, as appears above his head.

ay

A day is given to the tenants there to appoint a shepherd to keep watch over their animals before the feast of Corpus Christi (26th May), under penalty of $6^{s}8^{d}$.

rder

The order is given that none of the tenants there shall henceforth keep any sheepfold before the feast of *Saint* Michael (29th September) except those who had them from of old, because there are only three there, as they say, under penalty of 10^{s}.

preceptum — Preceptum est quod nulli Tenencium ibidem decetero loppabunt arbores ad faciendas cepes nisi ex assignacione ffirmarij ibidem sub pena iij^{s}iiij^{d}

dies — Jtem dicunt quod Johannes Makyn & Johannes Dawbern habent Canes qui occidunt Cuniculos domini Jdeo preceptum est eis dictos Canes interfecere vel eos extra dominium ponere citra festum pentecostes sub pena cuiuslibet eorum xij^{d}

ffiat accio — Jtem dicunt quod Johannes Bereman Bronn Vanriggon & petrus Bereman faciunt diuersas vias in terris domini Jdeo versus eos fiat Accio

dies — Preceptum est Thome Mores Molendario ibidem quod deinceps non transeat ultra grana Tenencium domini sub pena xij^{d}

Summa huius Curie xxij^{d}

der The order is given that none of the tenants there shall henceforth cut down trees to make hedges, except with the consent of the farmer there, under penalty of 3^s4^d. 1502

y Also, they say that John Makyn and John Dawbern have dogs which kill the lord's rabbits. Therefore the order is given them to kill the said dogs or put them outside the demesne before the feast of Pentecost (30th May), under penalty for each of them of 12^d.

tion to brought Also, they say that John Bereman, Bron Vanriggon and Peter Bereman make various roads on the lord's lands. Therefore let an action be brought against them.

y The order is given to Thomas Mores, miller there, that he shall not again take too much of the grain of the lord's tenants, under penalty of 12^d.

Amount of this court 22^d

Bandon — Cur*ia* ib*ide*m tent*a* die Jouis vicesimo septimo die april*is* anno r*egni* r*egis* henrici septimi decimo octauo

Essoni*um* — Null*um*

homagi*um* — Nich*ol*aus Waker, Thomas lews, Will*elmu*s legeard, Thomas hunt, Nich*ol*aus Glouer

Jur*ati*

Mi*sericordia* xvj[d] — Qui dic*unt* sup*er* Sacr*amentu*m suu*m* q*uo*d Rob*er*tus Morlay ar*miger* (ij[d]) Will*elmu*s lye valect*us* de Corona (ij[d]) Will*elmus* Batyson (ij[d]) Nich*ol*aus Burton de ffulh*a*m (ij[d]) Joh*ann*es Botery (ij[d]) Joh*ann*es haccher de Croydon (ij[d]) Joh*ann*es Waker (ij[d]) & Robert*us* holden (ij[d]) debent sect*am* Cur*ie* & fec*erunt* defalt*am* J*de*o ip*s*i in m*isericordia*

⌈Jt*e*m dic*unt* q*uo*d Joh*ann*es Payn qui de d*omi*no tenuit libere vnu*m* ten*ementum* cu*m* gardino adiacent*i* nup*er* Joh*ann*is payn & antea Wakers & quondam Cutbyes p*er* fidel*itatem* & redd*itum* xx[d] p*er* annu*m* & al*ia* s*er*uicia obijt inde Tenens sine hered*e* cit*ra* vlt*imam* Cur*iam* post cuius morte*m* n*ihi*l accid*it* d*omi*no de h*e*riett*o* q*uia* null*um* h*ab*uit a*n*imall & vlterius pr*eceptum* est balliuo intrare in dict*o* ten*emento* vt in escaeta sua Et vlt*e*rius pr*eceptum* est su*mmonere* Rob*er*tum Savage de Sutton qui illud tenet in iure Elene vx*or*is eius Tenent*is* p*ro* t*er*mino vite sue iux*ta* vlt*imam* voluntate*m* dic*ti* Joh*ann*is Payn sen*ioris* nup*er* viri p*re*dict*e* Elene⌋[1]

[1] This whole paragraph is cancelled.

Bandon A court held there on Thursday, the twenty-seventh day of April, in the eighteenth year of the reign of King Henry VII. 1503

Essoin None.

Homage

Homage	Nicholas Waker	Thomas Lews
	William Legeard	Thomas Hunt
	Nicholas Glover	

Sworn

Amercement 16^{d} These say on their oath that Robert Morlay, Esquire (2^{d}); William Lye, officer of the King's Chamber (2^{d}); William Batyson (2^{d}); Nicholas Burton of Fulham (2^{d}); John Botery (2^{d}); John Haccher of Croydon (2^{d}); John Waker (2^{d}) and Robert Holden (2^{d}) owe suit at court and have made default. Therefore they are in mercy.

/Also, they say that John Payn, who held freely of the lord a tenement with a garden adjacent, late of John Payn and earlier Waker's and before that Cutbye's, for fealty and a rent of 20^{d} a year and other services, has died tenant thereof without heir since the last court, after whose death nothing fell to the lord as heriot because there was no beast. And further, the order is given to the bailiff to enter the said tenement as in his own escheat. And further, the order is given to summon Robert Savage of Sutton, who holds it in right of Ellen his wife, tenant for the term of her life, according to the last wish of the said John Payn senior, late husband of the aforesaid Ellen./

Obit*us*

Jt*e*m dic*unt* q*uo*d Dionisia Newport de london vidua que de d*omi*no tenuit libere coniunctim in p*ro*p*er*tia cum Johanna Cooke p*er* ius accrescend*i* duas acras t*er*re vnde vna acra iacet in Cleyfurlong & altera iacet in le Shott voc*ata* Waddon marke vt filie & hered*es* Ric*ardi* Camberwell p*er* fidel*itatem* & r*edditum* viij^{d} p*er* an*num* & al*ia* s*er*uicia obijt inde sei*sit*a sine hered*e* cit*ra* vlt*imam* Cur*iam* post cuius morte*m* n*ihi*l accid*it* d*omi*no de h*er*iett*o* q*ui*a null*um* h*ab*uit a*nim*all   J*deo* pr*eceptum* est ball*io* intrare in dict*is* duab*us* acr*is* t*er*re vt in escaeta d*omi*ni & de exit*u* & c*etera*

escaeta d*omi*ni

Alienacio

Jt*e*m dic*unt* q*uo*d Joh*ann*es Best de Carsalton & lucia vx*or* eius qui de d*omi*no in iure d*ict*e lucie tenuer*unt* libere vnu*m* ten*ementum* cum gardino adiacent*i* nup*er* Will*elm*i aleyn & antea Thome aleyn & quond*am* allott*is* p*er* fidel*itatem* & Reddit*um* xij^{d} p*er* an*num* inde feoffauer*unt* Joh*ann*em Waker in feodo que*m* pr*eceptum* est dis*tringere* pr*o* fidel*itate*

fidelitas

Ad istam pr*eceptum* est ball*io* dis*tringere* Robert*um* Morley armigeru*m* p*ro* iij^{s}iiij^{d} Reddit*u* exeunt*i* de capit*itali* mess*uagio* modo in deiari*a* ac Cl*auso* & terr*is* in co*mmun*i Campo contin*enti* p*er* estimac*io*nem quin*qua*ginta acr*as* t*er*re ex confessione Ric*ard*i hiller ffirmarij inde vocat*o* Dogges   Necnon in alio ten*emento* in quo dict*us* Ric*ard*us hiller modo inh*ab*itat p*ar*cell*am* dict*i* Capit*ali*s mes*suagii*

Jt*e*m ordinatu*m* est ex assensu Tenenc*i*um q*uo*d

eath Also, they say that Dionisia Newport of London, widow, who held freely of the lord, conjointly in property with Joan Cooke by the law "Jus Accrescendi", as *they were* the daughters and heirs of Richard Camberwell, two acres of land, whereof one acre lies in Cleyfurlong and the other lies in le Shott called Waddon Marke, for fealty and a rent of 8^d a year and other services, has died seised thereof without heir since the last court. After her death nothing fell to the lord as heriot because she had no beast. Therefore the order is given to the bailiff to enter into the said two acres of land as into the lord's escheat, and of the consequences etc.. 1503

he lord's scheat

lienation Also, they say that John Best of Carshalton and Lucy his wife, who held freely of the lord, in right of the said Lucy, a tenement with a garden adjacent, late of William Aleyn and earlier of Thomas Aleyn and before that Allott's, for fealty and a rent of 12^d a year, have feoffed therein John Waker in fee. The order is given to distrain him for fealty.

ealty

At this *court* the order is given to the bailiff to distrain Robert Morley, Esquire, for 3^s4^d rent issuing from the capital messuage now in dairy and close and lands in the common field, containing by estimation fifty acres of land by the affirmation of Richard Hiller, farmer, *which was* then called Dogges, and also in another tenement in which the said Richard Hiller now inhabits a parcel of the said capital messuage.

Also, it is decreed, with the tenants' assent,

null*us* de cetero arabit siue harpicabit vlt*ra* fines t*errarum* sua*rum* cu*m* Carucis suis sub pen*a* cuiusl*ibe*t *pro* quol*ibet* def*e*ctu xx[d] leuari de bonis & Catall*is* suis ad opus d*omi*ni

Jt*e*m ordinat*um* est ex assensu Tenenc*i*um q*uo*d null*us* decetero ponet aliquos porcos in Co*mmun*ia d*omi*ni non annulat*os* siue /[justificatos]/ sub pe*na* cuiusl*ibe*t eo*rum* xx & q*uo*d null*us* decetero ponet in co*mmun*ib*us* Campis aliquas /[equas]/ sub pe*na* cuiusl*ibe*t eo*rum* xx[d] & q*uo*d null*us* de cetero frangat siue comburet cepes ib*ide*m sub pe*na* cuiusl*ibe*t eo*rum* xij[d]

Misericordia iij[s] — Jt*e*m dic*unt* q*uo*d Joh*ann*es Bereman de Croydon (xij[d]) petrus Bereman de Croydon (xij[d]) & Hans al*ias* Joh*ann*es pvirs de Croydon (xij[d]) indies cu*m* Carect*is* suis traseunt vlt*ra* terras d*omi*ni tales in le Westlond Bitmynges & Shortfurlong J*de*o ip*s*i in m*isericordia*

Misericordia vj[d] — Jt*e*m dic*unt* q*uo*d Ric*ar*dus aleyn (ij[d]) & vx*or* eius Thom*as* Jsak (ij[d]) & vx*or* eius Thom*as* laurence (ij[d]) & vx*or* eius indies frangunt & combustunt cepes ib*ide*m J*de*o ip*s*i in m*isericordia*

dis*tringere* — Pr*eceptum* est ball*io* dis*tringere* Will*elmu*m Batyson ad sect*am* Nich*ola*i Bolewyre ad ostenden*dum* quomo*do* tenet quin*que* acr*as* te*rre* pe*rtinentes* ten*emento* suo vocat*o* kytes prout p*ate*t per

that no one henceforth shall plough or harrow 1503
beyond the boundaries of his lands with his ploughs under penalty, for each and every one for each and every offence, of 20^{d} to be levied upon his goods and chattels for the use of the lord.

Also, it is decreed, with the tenants' assent, that no one henceforth shall put any pigs on the lord's common unringed or [unlicensed] under a penalty, for each and every one, of 20^{d}; and that no one henceforth shall put in the common fields any [mares] under a penalty, for each and every one of them, of 20^{d}; and that no one henceforth shall break down or burn the hedges there under a penalty, for each and every one of them, of 12^{d}.

Amercement 3^{s} Also, they say that John Bereman of Croydon (12^{d}), Peter Bereman of Croydon (12^{d}) and Hans, alias John, Pvirs of Croydon (12^{d}) cross the lord's lands daily with their carts in, for example, le Westland, Bitmynges and Shortfurlong. Therefore they are in mercy.

Amercement 6^{d} Also, they say that Richard Aleyn (2^{d}) and his wife, Thomas Isak (2^{d}) and his wife, Thomas Laurence (2^{d}) and his wife, daily break down and burn the hedges there. Therefore they are in mercy.

Distrain The order is given to the bailiff to distrain William Batyson at the suit of Nicholas Bolewyre to show by what right he holds five acres of land belonging to his tenement, called Kytes,

Cartam in Curia prolatam & ostensam

Obitus

Jtem presentant quod Johannes payn qui de domino tenuit libere sibi & helene uxori eius ad huc superstiti vnum tenementum cum gardino adjacenti ex dono & feoffamento Johannis Waker quondam Cutbyes per fidelitatem & redditum xx[d] per annum & alia seruicia obijt inde Tenens [1] sine herede citra ultimam Curiam post cuius mortem nihil accidit domino de herietto quia predicta helena dictum tenementum tenet per ius accrescendi pro termino vite sue Reuercionem inde domino feodali & heredibus suis [prospectiuis] Jdeo preceptum est Johanni Skete viro ipsius helene presenti hic in Curia Reparare tenementum predictum citra proximam Curiam sub pena [ ] [2]

heriettum nullum

dies

Affuratores Willelmus legeard Thomas huntt Jurati

[1] MS: Tenes

[2] Illegible.

as appears in the charter produced and shown in court. 1503

Death — Also, they present that John Payn who held freely of the lord, for himself and for Helen his wife at present surviving him, a tenement with a garden adjacent, formerly Cutbye's, by the gift and fief of John Waker, for fealty and a rent of 20^{d} a year and other services, has died tenant [1] thereof, without heir, since

No heriot — the last court. After his death nothing fell to the lord as heriot because the aforesaid Helen holds the said tenement by the law "Jus Accrescendi" for the term of her life, reversion thereof to the lord feudal and to his [prospective] heirs. Therefore the order is

Day — given to John Skete, the husband of the same Helen, present here in court, to repair the aforesaid tenement before the next court, under penalty of [ ]. [2]

Affeerers	William Legeard Thomas Huntt	Sworn

Bandon Curi*a* ib*ide*m tercio die Augusti anno re*gni* re*gis* henrici septimi decimo nono

Essoni*um* Null*um*

homagi*um*

Joh*annes* Waker	Thom*as* lews
Nich*ol*aus Waker	Thom*as* huntt
Wille*lmus* legeard	Joh*annes* Skete in Jure vx*or*is sue

Jur*a*t*i*

M*isericordia* xiiij^{d} Qui dic*unt* sup*er* Sacr*amentum* suu*m* qu*o*d Rob*er*tus Morley ar*miger* (ij^{d}) Wille*lmus* lye valect*us* de Corona (ij^{d}) Nich*ol*aus Burton de ffulh*am* (ij^{d}) Joh*annes* Boterye (ij^{d}) Joh*annes* haccher de Croydon (ij^{d}) Rob*er*tus holden (ij^{d}) Nich*ol*aus Glouer (ij^{d}) debent sect*am* Cur*ie* & fec*erunt* defalt*am* J*de*o ipsi in m*isericordia*

pr*eceptum* Pr*eceptum* est Joh*anni* Makyn (xx^{d}) Thome Jsak (xx^{d}) Rob*er*to Savage (xx^{d}) Joh*anni* Wodsett (xx^{d}) Nich*ol*ao Glouer (xx^{d}) & Joh*anni* Dawbern (xx^{d}) emere suffic*ientiam* ffocal*is* ad coburend*um* in domi*bus* suis cit*ra* fes*tum* s*an*cti Martini in yeme sic qu*o*d non capiant de cepibus aut subbosco d*omi*ni siue Tenenc*ium* v*idelicet* quil*ibe*t eo*rum* sub pe*na* p*rout* p*atet* in Capite

M*isericordia* iiij^{d} Jtem dic*unt* qu*o*d Joh*annes* Coyff (ij^{d}) & Thom*as* Galdewyn (ij^{d}) posuer*unt* equas suas in Co*mmuni* campo cont*ra* ordinac*io*nem inde prius fact*am* J*de*o ipsi in m*isericordia*

ndon

A court there on the third day of August in the nineteenth year of the reign of King Henry VII. 1504

ssoin

None

mage

John Waker	Thomas Lews
Nicholas Waker	Thomas Huntt
William Legeard	John Skete in right of his wife

Sworn

ercement 14^{d}

These say on their oath that Robert Morley, Esquire (2^{d}); William Lye, officer of the King's Chamber (2^{d}); Nicholas Burton of Fulham (2^{d}); John Boterye (2^{d}); John Haccher of Croydon (2^{d}); Robert Holden (2^{d}); Nicholas Glover (2^{d}), owe suit at court and have made default. Therefore they are in mercy.

der

The order is given to John Makyn (20^{d}), Thomas Isak (20^{d}), Robert Savage (20^{d}), John Wodsett (20^{d}), Nicholas Glover (20^{d}) and John Dawbern (20^{d}) to buy a sufficiency of fuel to burn in their homes before the feast of Saint Martin in the winter (11th November) so that they do not take from the hedges or underwood of the lord or the tenants. That is to say, each and every one of them is under a penalty as appears above his head.

ercement 4^{d}

Also, they say that John Coyff (2^{d}) and Thomas Galdewyn (2^{d}) have put their mares in the common field against the order concerning that *which was* made earlier. Therefore they are in mercy.

Obitus

Jtem dic*unt* q*uo*d Will*el*m*us* Batison qui de d*omi*no ten*ui*t libere duas dj*versas* acr*as* t*er*re in Bittnyng videl*ic*et de vtr*aque* p*ar*te Vni*us* dimidie acr*e* t*er*re Roberti Morley p*er* fidel*itatem* & reddit*um* ij^{d} p*er* an*num* Necnon tres acr*as* t*er*re nup*er* de ten*emento* Nich*ol*ai Glover p*er* fidel*itatem* & redd*itum* iij^{d} p*er* an*num* obijt inde tenens cit*ra* vltimam Cur*iam*

dis*tringere* p*ro* v^{d} de rel*ev*io & p*ro* fidel*itate*

post cui*us* mortem n*ihi*l accidit d*omi*no de h*er*iett*o* q*ui*a nullu*m* h*ab*uit a*n*im*a*l Et quis est eius p*ro*x*imus* heres ignorant q*ue*m prece*ptum* est distr*ingere* p*ro* fidel*itate* & v^{d} de Rel*ev*i*o*

Affur*atores* Joh*ann*es Waker / Nich*ol*aus Waker

ex*tracta*

S*um*m*a* huius Cur*ie* xviij^{d}

Death — Also, they say that William Batison, who held freely of the lord two separate acres of land in Bittnyng, that is to say on both sides of Robert Morley's half acre of land, for fealty and a rent of 2^d a year, and also three acres of land, recently *part* of Nicholas Glover's tenement, for fealty and a rent of 3^d a year, has died tenant thereof since the last court. After his death nothing fell to the lord as heriot because he had no beast. And they do not know who his next heir is who ought, as ordered, be distrained for fealty and 5^d for relief. 1504

Distrain for relief, 5^d, and for fealty

Affeerers John Waker
Nicholas Waker

Extracted

Amount of this court 18^d

Bandon	Cur*ia* ib*id*em tent*a* die Jouis p*roximo* post *fes*t*u*m Pasche v*idelicet* xxvij^{mo} die Marcij a*nn*o r*egni* r*egis* henrici Sept*imi* vicesimo
Essoni*um*	Null*um*
homagi*um*	Joh*ann*es Waker, Will*elmus* legeard, Thomas hunt, Thomas lewes, Nich*ol*aus Waker, Elena Skete — Jur*ati*
M*isericordia* xvj^{d}	Qui dic*unt* sup*er* sacr*amentum* suu*m* q*uo*d Robertus Morley armig*er* (iiij^{d}) Nich*ol*aus Burton de ffulh*a*m (ij^{d}) Joh*ann*es Botry (ij^{d}) Tenentes terr*e* nup*er* Will*elm*i Michell (ij^{d}) Tenens terr*e* nup*er* Dionisie Newport v*idelicet* Joh*ann*es Wody (ij^{d}) Tenens terr*e* nup*er* Will*elm*i Batyson (ij^{d}) & Joh*ann*es haccher de Croydon Colyer (ij^{d}) debent sect*am* Cur*ie* & fecer*unt* defalt*am* J*deo* ips*i* sep*ar*atim in m*isericord*ia
M*isericordia* vj^{d}	Nich*ol*aus Glouer (vj^{d}) in m*isericord*ia q*ui*a non ven*it* ad Warantizandum Essoniu*m* suu*m* de vlt*ima* Cur*ia* p*ro*ceden*s*
Alienac*io*	Jtem dic*unt* q*uo*d katerina Michell vidua nup*er* uxor Will*elm*i Michell que de d*omi*no libere tenet vnu*m* mes*suagium* & iiij^{xx} acr*as* terr*e* p*er* estimac*io*nem p*er* fidel*itatem* & redd*itum* ij^{s}iij^{d} p*er* annu*m* inde feoffauit Will*elmu*m Bonde in feod*o* Quiq*ui*dem Will*elmu*s immediate inde vlt*er*ius feoffauit Matheu*m* Broune Milite*m* Ric*ardu*m
dis*tringere* p*ro*	Guldeford Milite*m* Ric*ardu*m Marlond Gent*ilman* & alias tres p*er*sonas in feod*o* & *cetera* quos

Bandon A court held there on the Thursday next after the feast of Easter, that is to say on the 27th day of March, in the twentieth year of the reign of King Henry VII. 1505

Essoin None

Homage

John Waker	Thomas Lewes	
William Legeard	Nicholas Waker	Sworn
Thomas Hunt	Elena Skete	

Amercement 16^{d} These say on their oath that Robert Morley, Esquire (4^{d}); Nicholas Burton of Fulham (2^{d}); John Botry (2^{d}); the tenants of the land late of William Michell (2^{d}); the tenant of the land late of Dionisia Newport, that is to say John Wody (2^{d}); the tenant of the land late of William Batyson (2^{d}) and John Haccher of Croydon, collier (2^{d}), owe suit at court and have made default. Therefore they are severally in mercy.

Amercement 6^{d} Nicholas Glover (6^{d}) in mercy because he has not come to justify the essoin arising from the last court.

Alienation Also, they say that Katherine Michell, widow, late wife of William Michell, who holds freely of the lord a messuage and eighty acres of land by estimation for fealty and a rent of $2^{s}3^{d}$ a year, has feoffed therein William Bonde in fee. And the same William immediately further feoffed therein Matthew Broune, knight,

Distrain for Richard Guldeford, knight, Richard Marlond, gentleman, and three other persons in fee etc..

fidel*itate* — pr*eceptum* est distr*ingere* p*ro* fidel*itate* erga p*ro*x*imam* Cur*iam*

M*isericordia* xx^{d} — Jtem dic*unt* q*uo*d Robertus Savages (iiij^{d}) Joh*ann*es Watersale (iiij^{d}) Thomas Stapylhurst (iiij^{d}) Joh*ann*es Maken (iiij^{d}) & Joh*ann*es Wodesett (iiij^{d}) sunt Comm*un*es fractator*es* Cep*ium* Et Cepes illas asportant ad ignem J*de*o ip*s*i sep*ar*ati*m* in m*isericord*ia p*r*out p*atet* sup*er* eo*rum* Capit*a*

M*isericordia* ij^{s} — Jtem dic*unt* q*uo*d d*ic*tus Joh*ann*es Wodesett (ij^{s}) succidit duas vlnos in quod*a*m p*ar*vo Cl*aus*o p*er* mandat*um* vx*or*is d*omi*ni Et q*uo*d d*omi*n*us* h*abet* tres p*ar*uos Clausos quond*a*m edificat*os* iacent*es* ad d*omi*n*ium* Roberti Morley vocat*um* lokyers fealty — The order is given to distrain them for fealty by the next court. 1505

Amercement 20^d — Also, they say that Robert Savages (4^d), John Watersale (4^d), Thomas Stapylhurst (4^d), John Maken (4^d) and John Wodesett (4^d) are common breakers of hedges and that they carry off those hedges for firing. Therefore they are severally in mercy as appears above their heads.

Amercement 2^s — Also, they say that the said John Wodesett (2^s) cut down two elms in a certain little close by order of the wife of the lord and that the lord has three little closes, formerly enclosed, adjacent to the demesne of Robert Morley *which is* called Lokyers.

Bandon — Cur*i*a ib*i*de*m* tent*a* xvij^{o} die Septembr*is* Anno *regni regis* henrici septi*mi* xxj^{mo}

Essoni*um* — Null*um*

homagiu*m* — Joh*ann*es Waker Nich*ol*aus Waker
Thomas lewes Jur*ati*
Thomas hunt

M*isericordia* xviij^{d} — Qui dic*unt* sup*er* sacr*amentu*m suu*m* q*uo*d Robertus Morley Armiger (iiij^{d}) Elena Skete (ij^{d}) Nich*ol*aus Burton de ffulh*am* (ij^{d}) Joh*ann*es Botery (ij^{d}) Tenent*es* terr*e* nup*er* Will*elm*i Michell (ij^{d}) Tenens[2] terr*e* nup*er* Dionisie Newport v*idelicet* Joh*ann*es Wody (ij^{d}) Ten*ens* terr*e* nup*er* Will*elm*i Batysson (ij^{d}) Joh*ann*es haccher de Croydon Colyer (ij^{d}) d*eb*ent sect*am* Cur*ie* & fecer*unt* defalt*am* Curie J*de*o ips*i* in m*isericor*dia

M*isericordia* ij^{d} — Tenent*es* terr*e* nup*er* katerine Mychell (ij^{d}) in m*isericor*dia q*ui*a non ven*erunt* ad faciend*am* d*om*i*n*o fidel*itatem* & vlt*er*ius p*re*c*eptum* est

dis*tringere* — balli*o* distr*ingere* eos erga p*ro*x*imam* Cur*iam*

distr*ingere* — Ad huc p*re*c*eptum* est Balli*o* distr*ingere* Ten*entem* terr*e* nup*er* Will*elm*i Batyson p*ro* fidel*itate* & viij^{d} p*ro* Rel*e*vio erga p*ro*x*imam* Cur*iam*

Alienacio — Jtem dic*unt* q*uo*d Will*el*mus legger qui de

[2] MS: Tenent*es*

Bandon — A court held there on the 17th day of September in the twenty-first year of the reign of King Henry VII. 1505 [1]

Essoin — None

Homage — John Waker, Nicholas Waker, Thomas Lewes, Thomas Hunt — Sworn

Amercement 18d — These say on their oath that Robert Morley, Esquire (4d); Helen Skete (2d); Nicholas Burton of Fulham (2d); John Botery (2d); the tenants of land late of William Michell (2d); the tenant [2] of land late of Dionisia Newport, that is to say John Wody (2d); the tenant of land late of William Batysson (2d); John Haccher of Croydon, collier (2d), owe suit at court and have made default to the court. Therefore they are in mercy.

Amercement 2d — The tenants of land late of Katherine Mychell (2d) in mercy because they have not come to do fealty to the lord and, further, the order

Distrain — is given to the bailiff to distrain them by the next court.

Distrain — At this time the order is given to the bailiff to distrain the tenant of land late of William Batyson for fealty and 8d for relief by the next court.

Alienation — Also they say that William Legger, who held

[1] 1506? See above, p.vi at n.3.

d*omi*no tenuit libere vnu*m* ten*ementum* cu*m*
[gardino] & xxvj acr*as* terr*e* p*er* estimac*ion*em
quond*a*m Wellers p*er* fidel*itatem* & reddit*um*
ij^{s}ij^{d} inde feoffauit Robert*um* Jacson Carpenter

fidel*itas* Thomam huntt & Thomam Gryme & fecer*unt*
fidel*itatem*

Misericordia xl^{d} Jtem dic*unt* q*u*od Ph*ilipp*us Rowlond (xl^{d})
vicarius de Croydon sup*er*on*er*at Co*mmun*iam
d*omi*ni cu*m* equis porcis & aliis a*n*i*malib*us
J*de*o ipse in m*isericordi*a vel fiat acc*i*o

freely of the lord a tenement with [a garden] 1505
and twenty-six acres of land by estimation, formerly Weller's, for fealty and a rent of 2^s2^d, therein feoffed Robert Jacson, carpenter,

Fealty

Thomas Hunt and Thomas Gryme, and they did fealty.

Amercement
40^d

Also, they say that Philip Rowlond (40^d), vicar of Croydon, overloads the lord's common with horses, pigs and other animals. Therefore he is in mercy, or let an action be brought.

Bandon	Cur*ia* ib*ide*m tent*a* xxj^{o} die Augusti Anno regni Regis henrici septimi vicesimo s*e*c*un*do
Essoni*um*	Null*um*
Homagiu*m*	Joh*anne*s Waker Nich*ol*aus Waker Thomas lewes Nich*ol*aus Glouer Jur*ati*
M*isericordia* xx^{d}	Qui dic*unt* sup*er* sacr*amentu*m suu*m* q*uo*d Robertus Morley Armiger (iiij^{d}) Nich*ol*aus Burton de fullam (ij^{d}) Will*el*m*u*s legger (ij^{d}) Joh*anne*s Boterey (ij^{d}) tenen*tes* t*e*rr*e* Will*el*m*i* Bonde (ij^{d}) Joh*anne*s Wodey (ij^{d}) [ ] [1] Joh*anne*s haccher de Croydon (ij^{d}) & Thomas hunt (ij^{d}) de*b*ent sect*am* Cur*ie* & fecer*unt* defalt*am* Jd*e*o ips*i* in m*isericord*ia
dis*tringere* p*ro* fidel*itate*	Pr*ecep*t*um* est Ball*io* distr*ingere* Ten*entes* terr*e* nup*er* Katerine Michell postea Will*el*m*i* Bonde p*ro* fidel*itate* erga p*ro*x*imam* Cur*iam*
dis*tringere* p*ro* fidel*itate* p*ro* viij^{d} de rel*evio*	Ad huc p*r*e*ceptum* est Ball*io* distr*ingere* Ten*entem* terr*e* nup*er* Will*el*m*i* Batyson p*ro* fidel*itate* & viij^{d} p*ro* rel*ev*io erga p*ro*x*imam* Cur*iam*

Affur*atores* Joh*anne*s Waker
Nich*ol*aus Waker

S*umma* istar*um* triu*m* Cur*iarum* [ ]

[1] Erasure.

Bandon	A court held there on the 21st day of August in the twenty-second year of the reign of King Henry VII.	1507
Essoin	None	
Homage	John Waker Nicholas Waker Thomas Lewes Nicholas Glover Sworn	
Amercement 20^{d}	These say on their oath that Robert Morley, Esquire (4^{d}); Nicholas Burton of Fulham (2^{d}); William Legger (2^{d}); John Boterey (2^{d}); the tenants of William Bonde's land (2^{d}); John Wodey (2^{d}); [ ] [1] John Haccher of Croydon (2^{d}) and Thomas Hunt (2^{d}) owe suit at court and have made default. Therefore they are in mercy.	
Distrain for fealty	The order is given to the bailiff to distrain the tenants of land late of Katherine Michell, then of William Bonde, for fealty by the next court.	
Distrain for fealty and 8^{d} for relief	The order is given to the bailiff, at this time, to distrain the tenant of land late of of William Batyson for fealty and 8^{d} for relief by the next court.	

Affeerers   John Waker
Nicholas Waker

Amount of these three courts [ ]

Bandon — Cur*ia* Ric*ard*i Carewe Milit*is* ib*id*em tent*a* XIX° die Mens*is* Julij Anno r*egni* r*egis* henrici Sep*timi* vicesimo tercio

Essoni*um* — Nich*ol*aus Glover p*er* Joh*ann*em Waker Essoni*um* *est* de Co*mmuni* sect*a* Cur*ie*

homagi*um* — Joh*ann*es Waker, Thomas hunt, Will*el*m*us* legger, Nich*ol*aus Waker, Joh*ann*es Dawborne — Jur*ati*

M*isericordi*a xvj^{d} — Qui dic*unt* sup*er* sacr*amentu*m suu*m* q*uo*d Rob*er*tus Morley Armig*er* (iiij^{d}) Nich*ol*aus Burton de ffulh*a*m (ij^{d}) Joh*ann*es Boterey (ij^{d}) Will*el*m*us* Bonde Gent*ilman* (ij^{d}) Joh*ann*es Wodye (ij^{d}) Will*el*m*us* Batyson (ij^{d}) & Joh*ann*es haccher de Croydon (ij^{d}) deb*ent* sect*am* Cur*ie* & fecer*unt* defalt*am* J*de*o ip*s*i in m*isericord*ia

S*u*mm*a* xvj^{d}

Bandon

A court of Richard Carewe, knight, held there on the 19th day of the month of July in the twenty-third year of the reign of King Henry VII. 1508

Essoin

Nicholas Glover by John Waker: the essoin is of common suit of court.

Homage

John Waker	Thomas Hunt	
William Legger	Nicholas Waker	Sworn
John Dawborne		

Amercement 16d

These say on their oath that Robert Morley, Esquire (4^d); Nicholas Burton of Fulham (2^d); John Boterey (2^d); William Bonde, gentleman (2^d); John Wodye (2^d); William Batyson (2^d) and John Haccher of Croydon (2^d) owe suit at court and have made default. Therefore they are in mercy.

Amount 16^d

Bandon	Cur*ia* ib*id*em tent*a* xiiij^{o} die Junij anno regni Reg*is* henrici octaui pr*i*mo
Essoni*um*	Null*um*
homagiu*m*	Joh*annes* Waker Joh*annes* Dawborne Nich*ol*aus Waker Jur*ati* Wille*lmus* legger
M*isericordia* ij^{s}	Qui dic*unt* sup*er* Sacr*amentu*m suu*m* q*uo*d Rob*er*tus Morley armig*er* (iiij^{d}) Tenen*s* terr*e* nup*er* katerine Mychell (iiij^{d}) Joh*annes* Botery Gent*ilman* (iiij^{d}) Joh*annes* Wody Gent*ilman* (iiij^{d}) Tenen*s* terr*e* nup*er* Wille*lm*i Batyson (iiij^{d}) Thomas hunt (ij^{d}) & Joh*annes* haccher de Croydon (ij^{d}) debent sect*am* Cur*ie* & fecer*unt* defalt*am* J*de*o ip*s*i in m*isericordia*
ffin*is* sect*e* Cur*ie* iiij^{d}	Ad istam ven*it* Nich*ol*aus Burton de ffulh*am* (iiij^{d}) p*er* Thomam Whytehed attorn*atum* suu*m* & dat d*om*ino de ffin*e* p*ro* sect*a* Cur*ie* relax*ata* hoc anno instanti p*r*out p*atet* in Capite
Obitus h*er*iettu*m* j ouis p*r*ecii x^{d} dis*tringere* p*ro* rel*ev*io v*idelicet* iij^{d} & fidel*itate*	Comp*er*tu*m* est p*er* homagiu*m* q*uo*d Nich*ol*aus Glover qui de d*om*ino tenuit lib*er*e vnu*m* mes*suagium* cum gardino adiacen*ti* voc*atum* Kettis & tres acr*as* terr*e* diuisim iacen*tes* in Bandon feld p*er* fidel*itatem* & redditu*m* iij^{d} p*er* annu*m* diem suu*m* Clausit extremu*m* post cu*ius* morte*m* accidit d*om*ino de h*er*iett*o* vna Ouis p*r*ecij x^{d} Et vlt*er*ius dic*unt* q*uo*d Simon Glover est eius filius & heres & plene etat*is* Quem p*r*eceptu*m* est ballio distr*ingere* p*ro* iij^{d} de rel*ev*io & p*ro* fidel*itate* erga pro*x*i*mam* Cur*iam*

andon

A court held there on the 14th day of June in the first year of the reign of King Henry VIII. 1509

ssoin

None

omage

John Waker John Dawborne
Nicholas Waker Sworn
William Legger

iercement
2^{s}

These say on their oath that Robert Morley, Esquire (4^{d}); the tenant of land late of Katherine Mychell (4^{d}); John Botery, gentleman (4^{d}); John Wody, gentleman (4^{d}); the tenant of land late of William Batyson (4^{d}); Thomas Hunt (2^{d}) and John Haccher of Croydon (2^{d}) owe suit at court and have made default. Therefore they are in mercy.

.ne of
.it at
ourt 4^{d}

To this *court* comes Nicholas Burton of Fulham (4^{d}) by Thomas Whytehed his attorney and gives to the lord as a fine for suit at court remitted this current year as appears above his head.

ath

It is found by the homage that Nicholas Glover, who held freely of the lord a message with a garden adjacent called Kettis and three acres of land lying separately in Bandon Field for fealty and a rent of 3^{d} a year, has ended his days. After his death there fell to the lord as heriot a sheep worth 10^{d}. And further, they say that Simon Glover is his son and heir and of full age. The order is given to the bailiff to distrain him for relief, 3^{d}, and for fealty by the next court.

eriot
e sheep
rth 10^{d}
.strain
r relief
z. 3^{d}
d fealty

affur*atores* Joh*ann*es Waker
Nich*ol*aus Waker

S*umm*a hui*us* Cur*ie* iij^{s}v^{d}

Affeerers John Waker
Nicholas Waker

Amount of this court $3^s 5^d$

Bandon Curi*a* ib*i*d*e*m tent*a* xvij^{o} die Januarij anno regni Reg*is* henr*ici* viij s*ecun*do

Essoni*um* Null*um*

homagiu*m* Nich*ol*aus Waker Joh*ann*es Waker Wille*l*m*us* legger Thomas lewes Jur*ati*

M*i*s*eri*c*or*d*i*a xxij^{d} Qui dic*unt* sup*er* Sacr*amentu*m suu*m* q*uo*d Rob*er*tus Morley armig*er* (iiij^{d}) [1] Joh*ann*es Dawborn (iiij^{d}) Simon Glover (ij^{d}) Joh*ann*es Botery (iiij^{d}) Wille*l*m*us* Petley de halsted (ij^{d}) p*ro* ten*emento* nup*er* Wille*l*m*i* Bond Joh*ann*es Wody (ij^{d}) Rob*er*tus yate Consanguineus & heres Wille*l*m*i* Batyson (ij^{d}) & Thomas hunt (ij^{d}) sunt lib*er*i tenent*es* & [debent] sect*am* Cur*ie* & fecer*unt* defalt*am* Jd*e*o ips*i* sep*ar*ati*m* in m*i*s*eri*c*or*d*i*a

M*i*s*eri*c*or*d*i*a ix^{s}iiij^{d} Jt*em* p*re*sent*ant* q*uo*d Joh*ann*es hyller (iij^{s}iiij^{d}) succidit in cl*aus*o d*omi*ni vocat*o* Dryp*er*is unam Elme tree & sup*er* le Bank in Cullewylhawe ij Nuttrees & ij quarcos Et in Sandels Vnam quarcu*m* Jd*e*o ips*e* in m*i*s*eri*c*or*d*i*a & q*uo*d Joh*ann*es Watersale (viij^{d}) succidit in Cl*aus*o d*omi*ni q*uo*d tenet ad firmam vnam ulnu*m* Jd*e*o ips*e* & cetera ac eciam custodit vnu*m* feronem voc*atum* a fferrett in domo sua quem p*re*ceptum est Ballio eum accipere & q*uo*d Wille*l*m*us* Cogge (ij^{d}) succidit vnam magnam heythorn in le Comyn Heth ad nocument*um* Catall*i* tenenc*ium*

[1] Nich*ol*aus Burton de ffulham (iiij^{d}) cancelled.

andon A court held there on the 17th day of January in the second year of the reign of King Henry VIII. 1511

ssoin None

omage Nicholas Waker John Waker
William Legger Sworn
Thomas Lewes

ercement 22^d These say on their oath that Robert Morley, Esquire (4^d); [1] John Dawborn (4^d); Simon Glover (2^d); John Botery (4^d); William Petley of Halstead (2^d) for a tenement late of William Bond; John Wody (2^d); Robert Yate, kinsman and heir of William Batyson (2^d), and Thomas Hunt (2^d) are free tenants and [owe] suit at court and have made default. Therefore they are severally in mercy.

ercement 9^s4^d Also, they present that John Hyller (3^s4^d) cut down an elm tree in the lord's close, called Dryperis, and two nut trees and two oaks on le Bank in Cullewylhawe, and an oak in Sandels. Therefore he is in mercy.
And that John Watersale (8^d) cut down an elm in a close of the lord which he holds in farm. Therefore he etc.. And furthermore he keeps a "fero", called a ferret, in his house. The order is given to the bailiff to seize it.
And that William Cogge (2^d) cut down a big hawthorn on le Common Heath to the harm of

J*de*o ipse in m*iser*i*cord*ia & q*uo*d Joh*ann*es Stapyll (xl^{d}) succidit sup*er* le Downe Gosses & fyrres & eos vendidit inh*ab*itantibus de Carsalton ad nocument*um* tenenc*ium* d*omi*ni J*de*o ipse in m*iser*i*cord*ia & q*uo*d idem Joh*ann*es (viij^{d}) arrauit & versit le Worpyll cum arratris suis sic q*uo*d Tenen*tes* d*omi*ni non possunt venire ad terr*as* suas J*de*o ipse in m*iser*i*cord*ia & q*uo*d idem Joh*ann*es (xij^{d}) non sect*at* ad Molendinu*m* d*omi*ni ad dampnu*m* firmarij d*omi*ni d*i*cti Molendini & cont*ra* tenur*am* suam J*de*o ipse in m*iser*i*cord*ia & q*uo*d Joh*ann*es Watersall (ij^{d}) distruxit & fregit Cepes Nich*ol*ai Waker cum porcis suis J*de*o ipse in m*iser*i*cord*ia

Obitus	Comp*er*t*um* est p*er* homagiu*m* q*uo*d Nich*ol*aus Burton de ffulh*a*m qui de d*omi*no tenuit lib*er*e vnu*m* ten*emen*tu*m* & xiiij acr*as* terr*e* p*er* estimac*ionem* quond*a*m Russell*is* p*er* fidel*itatem* & reddit*um* v^{s} sect*am* Cur*ie* h*er*iett*um* & rel*ev*ium
h*er*iett*um* j equs p*re*cij xiij^{s}iiij^{d} distr*ingere* p*ro* v^{s} de rel*ev*io & fidel*itate*	cum accid*er*it diem suu*m* clausit extremu*m* post cui*us* mortem accid*it* d*omi*no de h*er*iett*o* vnus Equs p*re*cij xiij^{s}iiij^{d} & dic*unt* vlt*er*ius q*uo*d Thomas Burton est eius filius & heres & plene etatis Quem p*re*ceptu*m* est ballio distr*ingere* p*ro* v^{s} de rel*ev*io & fidel*itate* erga p*ro*x*i*m*am* Cur*iam*
alienac*io*	J*te*m p*re*sent*ant* q*uo*d Joh*ann*es haccher de Croydon Colyer qui de d*omi*no tenuit lib*er*e vnam acr*am* & dimid*iam* terr*e* sep*ar*ati*m* iacent*es* in Estlond*es* & butt[*antes*] sup*er* terr*am* archiepis*copi* Cantuar*ii* p*er* fidel*itatem* &

the tenants' cattle. Therefore he is in mercy. And that John Stapyll (40^{d}) cut gorse and furze on le Down and sold them to the inhabitants of Carshalton to the harm of the lord's tenants. Therefore he is in mercy. And that the same John (8^{d}) ploughed up and turned over le Worpyll with his ploughs so that the lord's tenants are not able to come to their lands. Therefore he is in mercy. And that the same John (12^{d}) does not take his grain to the lord's mill, to the loss of the lord's farmer of the said mill and against his tenure. Therefore he is in mercy. And that John Watersall (2^{d}) destroyed and broke down the hedges of Nicholas Waker with his pigs. Therefore he is in mercy. 1511

eath

It is found by the homage that Nicholas Burton of Fulham, who held freely of the lord a tenement and fourteen acres of land by estimation, late Russell's, for fealty and a rent of 5^{s}, suit at court, heriot, and relief when it falls due, has ended his days. After his death there fell to the lord as heriot a horse worth $13^{s}4^{d}$. And they further say that Thomas Burton is his son and heir and of full age. The order is given to the bailiff to distrain him for relief, 5^{s}, and fealty by the next court.

eriot
ne horse
orth $13^{s}4^{d}$
istrain for
elief of 5^{s}
nd fealty

lienation

Also, they present that John Haccher of Croydon, collier, who held freely of the lord an acre and a half of land lying separately in Eastlands and abutting on the Archbishop of Canterbury's land, for fealty and a rent of

	redditum iij[d] per annum sectam Curie heriettum & relevium cum acciderit inde feoffauit
distringere pro fidelitate	Johannem Boterys & alios in feodo quos preceptum est ballio distringere pro fidelitate erga proximam Curiam
alienacio	Jtem dicunt quod Willelmus Bond qui de domino tenuit libere vnum tenementum & diuersas terras nuper Mychels per fidelitatem & redditum ij[s]iij[d] sectam Curie heriettum & relevium cum acciderit inde feoffauit Willelmum
distringere pro fidelitate	Petley de halsted in Comitatu kancio in feodo quem preceptum est ballio distringere pro fidelitate erga proximam Curiam

afferatores: Willelmus leger, Johannes Waker

Summa huius Curie xxix[s]vj[d]

	3^d a year, suit at court, heriot, and relief when it falls due, has feoffed therein John	1511
Distrain for fealty	Boterys and others in fee. The order is given to the bailiff to distrain them for fealty by the next court.	
Alienation	Also, they say that William Bond, who held freely of the lord a tenement and various lands, late Mychel's, for fealty and a rent of 2^s3^d, suit at court, heriot, and relief when it falls due, has feoffed therein William	
Distrain for fealty	Petley of Halstead in the County of Kent in fee. The order is given to the bailiff to distrain him for fealty by the next court.	

Affeerers William Leger, John Waker

Amount of this court 29^s6^d

Bandon	Cur*i*a ib*i*d*e*m tent*a* xxviij^{o} die Septembr*is* Anno r*egni* r*egis* henr*ici* viij^{ui} te*r*cio
Essoni*um*	Null*um*
homagi*um*	Nich*ol*aus Waker Wille*l*m*us* legger Joh*ann*es Waker Thomas lewes Jur*ati* Joh*ann*es Dawborn
Misericordia iij^{s}iiij^{d}	Qui dic*unt* sup*er* Sacr*amentu*m suu*m* q*uo*d Robe*r*tus Morley armig*er* (viij^{d}) Thomas Burton de ffulh*am* (iiij^{d}) Joh*ann*es Botery (viij^{d}) Wille*l*m*us* Petley de halsted (viij^{d}) Joh*ann*es Wodye (ij^{d}) Robe*r*tus yates de london draper (viij^{d}) & Thomas huntt (ij^{d}) debent sect*am* Cur*i*e & fecer*unt* defalt*am* J*de*o ip*s*i in m*isericord*ia

affur*atores* Nich*ol*aus Waker
Thomas lewes

S*umma* hui*us* Cur*i*e iij^{s}iiij^{d}

andon — A court held there on the 28th day of September in the third year of the reign of King Henry VIII. — 1511[1]

ssoin — None

omage

Nicholas Waker	William Legger	
John Waker	Thomas Lewes	Sworn
John Dawborn		

mercement 3^s4^d — These say on their oath that Robert Morley, Esquire (8^d); Thomas Burton of Fulham (4^d); John Botery (8^d); William Petley of Halstead (8^d); John Wodye (2^d); Robert Yates of London, draper (8^d), and Thomas Huntt (2^d) owe suit at court and have made default. Therefore they are in mercy.

Affeerers: Nicholas Waker, Thomas Lewes

Amount of this court 3^s4^d

[1] 1512? See above, p.vi at n.3.

Bandon	Cur*i*a ib*i*dem tent*a* xx^{o} die Januarij anno regni Re*gis* henr*ici* viij quarto
Esson*i*um	Null*um*
homagium	Nicho*la*us Waker Thomas hunt Thomas lewes Joh*ann*es Waker Joh*ann*es Dawborn Rob*er*tus yates Wille*l*m*u*s legger Jur*ati*
M*isericordia* ij^{s}	Qui dic*unt* sup*er* Sacr*amentum* suu*m* q*uo*d Rob*er*tus Morley armig*er* (iiij^{d}) Thomas Burton de ffulh*am* (iiij^{d}) Simon Glover (iiij^{d}) Joh*ann*es Botery (iiij^{d}) Wille*l*m*us* Petley de halsted (iiij^{d}) & Joh*ann*es Wody (iiij^{d}) debent sect*am* Cur*i*e & fecer*unt* defalt*am* Jd*e*o ip*s*i in m*iser*i*cord*ia
ffin*is* sect*e* Cur*i*e iiij^{d}	Ad istam ven*it* Rob*er*tus yates (iiij^{d}) & dat d*omi*no de ffin*e* p*ro* sect*a* Cur*ie* relax*ata* hoc anno p*ro*ut p*atet* in Capite

Affur*atores* Joh*ann*es Waker
Thomas huntt

S*umma* huius Cur*ie* ij^{s}iiij^{d}

Bandon — A court held there on the 20th day of January in the fourth year of the reign of King Henry VIII. 1513

Essoin — None

Homage

Nicholas Waker	Thomas Hunt	Thomas Lewes
John Waker	John Dawborn	
Robert Yates	William Legger	

Sworn

Amercement 2^{s} — These say upon their oath that Robert Morley, Esquire (4^{d}); Thomas Burton of Fulham (4^{d}); Simon Glover (4^{d}); John Botery (4^{d}); William Petley of Halstead (4^{d}) and John Wody (4^{d}) owe suit at court and have made default. Therefore they are in mercy.

Fine of suit at court 4^{d} — To this *court* comes Robert Yates (4^{d}) and gives to the lord as fine for suit at court remitted this year as appears above his head.

Affeerers: John Waker, Thomas Huntt

Amount of this court $2^{s}4^{d}$

Bandon — Curia Ric*ardi* Carewe Militis ib*idem* tent*a* xxiiij^{o} die Septembr*is* anno regni Regis henrici octaui sexto

Essoni*um* — Null*um*

homagi*um* — Nich*ol*aus Waker, Joh*ann*es Waker, Wille*lm*us legger, Thomas lewes, Wille*lm*us Wylkynson in Jure Joh*ann*e vx*or*is eius, Simon Glover

Jur*ati*

Misericordia ij^{s} — Qui dic*unt* sup*er* sacr*amentu*m suu*m* q*uo*d Robertus Morley armig*er* (iiij^{d}) Thomas Burton de ffulh*a*m (iiij^{d}) Joh*ann*es Botery (iiij^{d}) Wille*lm*us petley de halsted (iiij^{d}) Joh*ann*es Wody (iiij^{d}) & Thomas hunt (iiij^{d}) debent sect*am* Cur*ie* & fec*erunt* defalt*am* J*de*o ip*s*i sep*a*ratim in *misericord*ia

Misericordia iiij^{d} — Jt*e*m p*re*sent*ant* q*uo*d Thomas Brampton (iiij^{d}) Amputauit ramos vni*us* arboris crescen*tis* sup*er* leggerhyll sine licencia J*de*o ip*s*e in *misericord*ia

Misericordia iiij^{d} — Jt*e*m dic*unt* q*uo*d Thomas hyller (iiij^{d}) accrochiauit terr*as* p*er*tinent*es* ten*emento* nup*er* Wille*lm*i Batysons v*idelicet* vj pedes cum aratro suo ex vtraq*ue* p*ar*te terr*e* sue ib*idem* J*de*o ip*s*e in *misericord*ia

fidel*itas* — Ad istam venit Simon Glover filius & heres Nich*ol*ai Glover & fec*it* dom*i*no fidel*itatem* p*ro* j mes*suagio* Gardino & iij acr*is* terr*e*

Bandon — A court of Richard Carewe, knight, held there on the 24th day of September in the sixth year of the reign of King Henry VIII. 1514

Essoin — None

Homage — Nicholas Waker, John Waker, William Legger, Thomas Lewes, William Wylkynson in right of his wife Joan, Simon Glover

Sworn

Amercement 2s — These say on their oath that Robert Morley, Esquire (4d); Thomas Burton of Fulham (4d); John Botery (4d); William Petley of Halstead (4d); John Wody (4d) and Thomas Hunt (4d) owe suit at court and have made default. Therefore they are severally in mercy.

Amercement 4d — Also, they present that Thomas Brampton (4d) cut off, without licence, the branches of a tree growing on Legger Hill. Therefore he is in mercy.

Amercement 4d — Also, they say that Thomas Hyller (4d) encroached upon lands belonging to the tenement late of William Batyson, that is to say six feet with his plough on either side of his land in that same place. Therefore he is in mercy.

Fealty — To this *court* came Simon Glover, son and heir of Nicholas Glover, and did fealty to the lord for a messuage, a garden and three acres of

Rel*evium* vad*iavit* ij^{d}	jac*entibus* in Bandon voc*atis* kettes nup*er* d*ic*ti Nich*ol*ai pa*t*ris sui & vad*iavit* rel*evium* suu*m* videl*ic*et ij^{d}
Obitus h*er*iett*um* j vacc*a* precii vj^{s}viij^{d} fidel*itas* rel*evium* ij^{s}ij^{d} vad*iavit*	Jt*e*m p*r*esent*ant* q*uo*d Will*el*m*us* legger qui de d*omi*no tenuit lib*er*e j ten*ementum* cum gardino & xxvj acras terr*e* p*er* estimac*ionem* p*er* fidel*itatem* & redd*itum* ij^{s}ij^{d} sect*am* Cur*ie* h*er*iett*um* & rel*evium* cum accid*erit* obijt inde tenens cit*ra* vlt*imam* Cur*iam* post cui*us* mortem accid*it* d*omi*no j vacca p*r*ecij vj^{s}viij^{d} & vlt*er*ius dic*unt* q*uo*d Will*el*m*us* legger e*st* eius filius & heres & plene etat*is* Quiquidem Will*el*m*us* p*r*esens in Cur*ia* fec*it* do*mi*no fidel*itatem* & vadiauit Rel*e*uium suu*m* v*idelicet* ij^{s}ij^{d}
Obitus h*er*iett*um* j vacc*a* p*r*ecii vij^{s} rel*evium* xx^{d} vad*iavit* fidel*itas* rem*anet*	Jt*e*m p*r*esent*ant* q*uo*d Joh*ann*es Dawborn qui de d*omi*no tenuit lib*er*e j ten*ementum* cum Gardino adjacent*i* p*er* fidel*itatem* & redd*itum* xx^{d} sect*am* Cur*ie* h*er*iett*um* & rel*evium* cum accid*erit* obijt inde tenens cit*ra* vlt*imam* Cur*iam* post cui*us* mortem accid*it* d*omi*no de h*er*iett*o* j vacca p*r*ecii vij^{s} & vlt*er*ius dic*unt* q*uo*d Johanna nup*er* ux*or* d*icti* Joh*ann*is & modo ux*or* Will*el*m*i* Wylkynson h*a*bet p*r*edict*um* ten*ementum* cum Gardino p*r*o t*er*m*i*no vite sue & insup*er* dic*unt* q*uo*d Rob*er*tus Dawborn est eius filius sen*ior* & heres & est etat*is* ix anno*rum* Quiquidem Will*el*m*us* Wylkynson vadiauit rel*e*vium suu*m* videlicet xx^{d} & fidel*itas* d*icti* Rob*er*ti rem*anet*
Alienac*io*	Jt*e*m p*r*esent*ant* q*uo*d Joh*ann*es haccher de Croydon Colyer qui de d*omi*no tenuit lib*er*e j

Relief paid 2^d

land lying in Bandon, called Kettes, late of 1514
the said Nicholas, his father. And he paid his relief, namely 2^d.

Death
Heriot one cow worth 6^s8^d
Fealty
Relief 2^s2^d paid

Also, they present that William Legger, who held freely of the lord a tenement with a garden and twenty-six acres of land by estimation for fealty and a rent of 2^s2^d, suit at court, heriot, and relief when it falls due, has died tenant thereof since the last court. After his death there fell to the lord a cow worth 6^s8^d. And further, they say that William Legger is his son and heir and of full age. And the same William, present in court, did fealty to the lord and paid his relief, namely 2^s2^d.

Death
Heriot one cow worth 7^s
Relief 20^d paid
Fealty respited

Also, they present that John Dawborn, who held freely of the lord a tenement with a garden adjacent for fealty and a rent of 20^d, suit at court, heriot, and relief when it falls due, has died tenant thereof since the last court. After his death there fell to the lord as heriot a cow worth 7^s. And further, they say that Joan, late wife of the said John and now wife of William Wylkynson, has the aforementioned tenement with garden for the term of her life. And, moreover, they say that Robert Dawborn is her eldest son and heir and is nine years old. The same William Wylkynson paid his relief, namely 20^d, and the fealty of the said Robert is respited.

Alienation

Also, they say that John Haccher of Croydon, collier, who held freely of the lord an acre acr*am* & di*midiam* terr*e* quond*am* Norfolk*is* p*er* fidel*itatem* & reddit*um* [1] iij[d] sect*am* Cur*ie* & rel*evium* cum accid*erit* inde ffeoffauit Joh*ann*em Botery in feod*o* quem p*re*ceptu*m* est Ballio distr*ingere* p*ro* fidel*itate* erga p*ro*x*imam* Cur*iam*

1 MS: rel*evium*

and a half of land, formerly Norfolk's, for 1514
fealty and a rent [1] of 3^d, suit at court and relief when it falls due, has feoffed therein John Botery in fee. The order is given to the bailiff to distrain him for fealty by the next court.

Bandon	Cur*ia* Ric*ardi* Carew Milit*is* tent*a* ib*idem* tercio die Januarij anno regni Regis henr*ici* Octaui decimo
Esson*ium*	Null*um*
M*isericord*ia xx^d	Homagiu*m* ib*idem* videl*ic*et Joh*ann*es Waker Thomas hunt Nich*ol*aus Waker Will*elmu*s legger & Simon Glover qui Jur*ati* p*re*sent*ant* q*uo*d Will*elmu*s Petley (iiij^d) alicia Morley (viij^d) Joh*ann*es Botery (iiij^d) & tenen*s* terr*e* nup*er* [ ] May (iiij^d) sunt sect*atores* Cur*ie* & fac*iunt* def*altam* *ide*o ip*s*i rem*anent* in M*isericord*ia p*ro*ut patet sup*er* eo*rum* Capita
pena for*is* xx^d	Jt*e*m p*re*sent*ant* q*uo*d henricus hudson (xx^d) qui h*ab*uit pena*m* q*uo*d ip*s*e a dat*o* vlt*ime* Cur*ie* non transit cu*m* bigis suis vlt*ra* terr*as* Nich*ol*ai Waker iacent*es* in Cleyfurlong m*od*o dic*unt* homagiu*m* q*uo*d ip*s*e diu*ers*is temp*or*ibu*s* ex quo transiuit vlt*ra* p*re*dict*as* terr*as* cu*m* bigis suis sine licencia ip*s*ius Nich*ol*ai *ide*o incurr*it* pena*m* p*ro*ut patet sup*er* eius Caput
Fin*is* viij^d	Jt*e*m p*re*sent*ant* q*uo*d Ric*ard*us Wright (viij^d) succidit vna*m* vln*u*m in terr*a* d*omi*ni iacent*i* iuxta ten*emen*tum in quo idem Ric*ard*us m*od*o inh*ab*itat & idem Ric*ard*us inde allocut*us* cogn*ovit* tr*a*nsgr*essionem* & pon*it* se in grac*ia* d*omi*ni vnde fin*is* p*ro*ut patet sup*er* eius Caput

Bandon — A court of Richard Carew, knight, held there on the 3rd day of January in the tenth year of the reign of King Henry VIII. 1519

Essoin — None

Amercement 20^{d} — The homage there, namely: John Waker, Thomas Hunt, Nicholas Waker, William Legger and Simon Glover, who, being sworn, present that William Petley (4^{d}), Alice Morley (8^{d}), John Botery (4^{d}) and the tenant of land late of [ ] May (4^{d}) are suitors at court and make default. Therefore they remain in mercy as appears above their heads.

Penalty for outdoor offences 20^{d} — Also, they present that Henry Hudson (20^{d}) had a penalty that he, from the date of the last court, should not encroach with his carts on the lands of Nicholas Waker lying in Cleyfurlong: now the homage say that he at various times since then has encroached on the aforementioned lands with his carts without licence of the same Nicholas, therefore he incurs the penalty as appears above his head.

Fine 8^{d} — Also, they present that Richard Wright (8^{d}) cut down an elm in land of the lord lying next to the tenement in which the same Richard now lives, and the same Richard questioned thereon has acknowledged his transgression and places himself in the grace of the lord whence the fine as appears above his head.

affur*atores* Nich*ol*aus Waker, Joh*annes* Waker Jur*ati*

S*umma* hui*us* Cur*ie* iiij[s]

Affeerers	Nicholas Waker John Waker	Sworn	1519

Amount of this court 4^s

Bedyngton

Cur*ia* Ric*ard*i Carew Milit*is* tent*a* ib*ide*m tercio die Januarij anno regni Regis henr*ici* Octaui decimo

Essoni*um*

Null*um*

Mi*sericord*ia
xvj^{d}

Homag*ium* ib*ide*m videl*ice*t Thomas hunt Joh*ann*es Bristowe de logge, Thomas hewett & henr*icus* Stapehurst qui Jur*ati* p*resentant* q*uo*d Joh*ann*es Skynner (iiij^{d}) p*ri*or de Reygate (iiij^{d}) Joh*ann*es Codyngton de Codyngton (iiij^{d}) tenen*s* terr*e* nup*er* Joh*ann*is pope (iiij^{d}) sunt sect*atores* Cur*ie* & fac*iunt* def*altam* i*de*o ip*s*i rem*anent* in Mi*sericord*ia p*ro*ut patet sup*er* eo*rum* Capita

Alienac*io*

Jt*e*m p*resentant* q*uo*d Joh*ann*es Staplehurst qui de d*omi*no tenuit lib*er*e cert*as* terr*as* voc*atas* le West lond p*er* reddit*um* ij^{s}xj^{d} p*er* ann*um* p*re*missa vendidit henr*ico* Staplehurst qui quidem Henr*icus* p*re*sens in Cur*ia* cogn*ovit* teneri p*redi*ctas terr*as* de d*omi*no p*er* p*redictum* reddit*um* sect*am* Cur*ie* & al*ia* & ce*tera* & ffecit d*omi*no ffidelit*atem*

ffidelit*as*

obitus

Jt*e*m p*resen*t*ant* q*uo*d Joh*ann*es Skynner qui de d*omi*no tenuit lib*er*e duos Campos terr*e* un*de* vn*us* campus voc*atus* Newfeld & alius voc*atus* Strodefeld iacent*es* iuxta Bentyngwode obijt ante hanc Cur*iam* & q*uo*d ip*s*e ante mortem suam inde int*er* al*ia* feoffauit Will*elm*um Merston & al*ios* ad vsum Joh*ann*is Skynner ffilij & hered*is* apparent*is* & kat*er*ine ux*or*is sue p*ro* t*er*mino vite sue & post eo*rum* decessum

Beddington — A court of Richard Carew, knight, held there on the 3rd day of January in the tenth year of the reign of King Henry VIII. 1519

Essoin — None

Amercement 16d — The homage there, namely Thomas Hunt, John Bristow of Logge, Thomas Hewett and Henry Stapehurst, who, being sworn, present that John Skynner (4d), the Prior of Reigate (4d), John Codyngton of Codyngton (4d), the tenant of land late of John Pope (4d) are suitors at court and make default. Therefore they remain in mercy as appears above their heads.

Alienation — Also, they present that John Staplehurst, who held freely of the lord certain lands called Le West Land for a rent of 2s11d a year, has sold the premises to Henry Staplehurst, and the same Henry, present in court, has acknowledged that the aforementioned lands are held of the lord for the aforementioned

Fealty — rent, suit at court and other etc.. And he did fealty to the lord.

Death — Also, they present that John Skynner, who held freely of the lord two fields , one field called New Field and the other called Strode Field, lying next to Bentyngwode, died before this court; and that he, before his death, feoffed therein, amongst other things, William Merston and others to the use of John Skynner, his son and heir apparent, and of Katherine, his wife, for the term of their life and after

ad vsum suum proprium & heredum suorum per cuius mortem accidit domino de herietto vnus

heriettum — bos & pro relevio & ffidelitate preceptum

Distringere — est ballio quod distringat Johannem Skynner ffilium domino accidentibus per mortem patris sui citra proximam Curiam

obitus — Jtem presentant quod Johannes pope senior de Wodehacch qui de domino tenuit libere certas parcellas terre per redditum [ ] per annum obijt ante hanc Curiam & quod ipse ante mortem suam inde ffeoffauit Johannem Skynner & alios ad eius vsum & heredum suorum per cuius mortem accidit domino de herietto vnus bos precij xij^s qui deliberatus fuit domino & quod Johannes Pope fuit ffilius & heres predicti Johannis & plene etatis qui similiter obijt ante hanc Curiam per cuius mortem accidit

heriettum xxiiij^s — domino de herietto vnus alius bos precii xij^s qui similiter deliberatus fuit domino & ante mortem suam voluit per vltimam voluntatem suam quod Margareta vxor sua habeat & gaudiat predictas terras inter alia pro termino vite sue & post eius decessum omnia premissa remaneant Johanni pope ffilio & heredi dicti Johannis pope & heredibus suis imperpetuum & ideo preceptum est Ballio quod distringat

Distringere — tenentem & occupat premissa tam pro Relevio domino accidenti per mortem Johannis pope senioris quam pro Relevio & ffidelitate domino accidentibus per mortem Johannis pope filij sui citra proximam Curiam

their decease to his own use and that of his heirs. By his death there fell to the lord as heriot an ox. And the order is given to the bailiff to distrain John Skynner, the son, before the next court for the relief and fealty falling due to the lord through the death of his father. 1519

Heriot

Distrain

Death

Also, they present that John Pope senior of Woodhatch, who held freely of the lord certain parcels of land for a rent of [ ] a year, died before this court; and that he, before his death, therein feoffed John Skynner and others to his use and that of his heirs. After his death there fell to the lord as heriot an ox worth 12^s which was delivered to the lord. And that John Pope was the son and heir of the aforementioned John and of full age, who likewise died before this Court. By his death there fell to the lord as heriot another ox worth 12^s which was likewise delivered to the lord. And before his death he wished as his last wish that Margaret his wife should have and enjoy the aforementioned lands, amongst others, for the term of her life, and after her decease all the premises should remain to John Pope, the son and heir of the said John Pope, and to his heirs for ever. And therefore the order is given to the bailiff to distrain the tenant and occupy the premises, both for the relief falling due to the lord by the death of John Pope senior and for the relief and fealty falling due to the lord by the death of John Pope his son, before the next court.

Heriot 24^s

Distrain

obitus

J*te*m p*resentant* q*uo*d Joh*ann*es Robson p*ri*or p*ri*orat*us* de Reygate qui de d*omi*no tenuit lib*e*re cert*as* terr*as* vocat*as* [ ] p*er* reddit*um* xviij^{d} p*er* annu*m* obijt diu ante hanc Cur*iam* p*er* cui*us* morte*m* accid*it* d*omi*no de h*er*iett*o* [ ] & q*uo*d postea elect*us* fuit p*ri*or p*ri*oratus p*redic*ti quem p*re*cept*um* est distr*ingere* p*ro* h*er*iett*o*

Distr*ingere*

Relevio & ffidelit*ate* d*omi*no debit*is* p*er* morte*m* p*re*decess*oris* sui cit*ra* p*roximam* Cur*iam*

Alienac*io*

J*te*m p*resentant* q*uo*d laurenc*ius* Gylemer Miles qui de d*omi*no tenuit lib*e*re cert*as* terr*as* & ten*emen*ta voc*ata* [ ] quiquidem laurenc*ius* p*re*missa alienauit Nich*ol*ao Carew que*m* p*re*cept*um* est distr*ingere* p*ro* ffidelit*ate*

distr*ingere*

cit*ra* p*roximam* Cur*iam*

affur*atores* Joh*ann*es Bristow / Henr*icus* Staplehurst Jur*ati*

S*umma* hui*us* Cur*ie* xxv^{s}iiij^{d}

Death — Also, they present that John Robson, prior of the priory of Reigate, who held freely of the lord certain lands called [ ] for a rent of 18^{d} a year, died long before this court; by whose death there fell to the lord as heriot [ ] : and that afterwards a prior of the aforementioned priory was elected. The order is given to distrain him for the heriot, relief and fealty due to the lord by the death of his predecessor before the next court. 1519

Distrain

Alienation — Also, they present that Laurence Gylemer, knight, held freely of the lord certain lands and tenements called [ ] and the same Laurence alienated the premises to Nicholas Carew. The order is given to distrain him for fealty before the next court.

Distrain

Affeerers John Bristow, Henry Staplehurst Sworn

Amount of this court 25^{s}4^{d}

Bandon — *Curia Ricardi* Carew *Militis* tent*a* ib*idem* quinto die Marcij anno regni Regis henrici Octavi undecimo

Esson*ium* — Null*um*

Misericordia xviij^{d} — Homag*ium* ib*idem* videl*icet* Nich*olaus* Waker Will*elmus* legger Simon Glover & Henr*icus* Shott qui Jur*ati* *presentant* qu*od* Thomas hunt (ij^{d}) alic*ia* Morley vidua (vj^{d}) Joh*ann*es Botery (iiij^{d}) Will*elmus* petley (iiij^{d}) tenen*s* terr*e* [ ] May (ij^{d}) sunt sect*atores* Cur*ie* & ffac*iunt* def*altam* sect*e* id*eo* ips*i* rem*anent* in *Misericordia* pr*o*ut patet sup*er* eo*rum* Capit*a*

obitus — Jt*em* *presentant* qu*od* Joh*ann*es Waker qui de d*omi*no tenuit libere vnu*m* ten*emen*tu*m* & vnu*m* gardinu*m* & dimid*iam* acr*am* terr*e* nup*er* Will*elm*i Mokell p*er* redditu*m* xx^{d} p*er* annu*m* & vnu*m* ten*emen*tu*m* & xiiij acr*as* terr*e* nup*er* Rob*er*ti Russell p*er* redditu*m* v^{s} p*er* annu*m* & cert*as* terr*as* iacen*tes* ex p*ar*tibu*s* boriali & australi vniu*s* ten*emen*ti nup*er* Thome holden cont*inentes* ij acr*as* & d*imidiam* terre p*er* redditu*m* xij^{d} p*er* annu*m* que tenent*ur* in escambiu*m* & p*redi*ctu*m* ten*emen*tu*m* nup*er* Thome holden p*er* redditu*m* xviij^{d} p*er* annu*m* & vna*m* acra*m* & dimid*iam* terr*e* nup*er* Rob*er*ti Wannell p*er* redditu*m* ij^{d} obijt post vlti*m*am Cur*iam* inde seis*itus* p*er* cuiu*s* morte*m* accidit d*omi*no

h*er*iett*um* lv^{s} — de h*er*iett*o* duos Equos utriusq*ue* eo*rum* p*re*cij xx^{s} & vnu*m* bouem p*re*cij xv^{s} videl*icet* p*ro* quoli*bet* ten*emen*to vnu*m* h*er*iett*um* Et qu*od* Rob*er*tus Waker est ffilius & heres p*redicti*

Bandon — A court of Richard Carew, knight, held there on the 5th day of March in the eleventh year of the reign of King Henry VIII. 1520

Essoin — None

Amercement 18d — The homage there, namely: Nicholas Waker, William Legger, Simon Glover and Henry Shott, who, being sworn, present that Thomas Hunt (2d); Alice Morley, widow (6d); John Botery (4d); William Petley (4d); the tenant of land of [ ] May (2d) are suitors at court and make default of suit. Therefore they remain in mercy as appears above their heads.

Death — Also, they present that John Waker, who held freely of the lord a tenement and a garden and half an acre of land, late of William Mokell, for a rent of 20d a year; and a tenement and fourteen acres of land, late of Robert Russell, for a rent of 5s a year; and certain lands, lying on the north and south sides of a tenement late of Thomas Holden, containing two and a half acres of land, for a rent of 12d a year, which are held in exchange; and the aforesaid tenement, late of Thomas Holden, for a rent of 18d a year, and one and a half acres of land, late of Robert Wannell, for a rent of 2d, has died since the last court seised thereof. By his death there fell to the lord

Heriot 55s — as heriot two horses, each of them worth 20s, and one ox worth 15s: that is to say, for each tenement a heriot. And that Robert Waker is the son and heir of the aforementioned John

relevium $ix^{s}iiij^{d}$ ffidelit*as* — Joh*ann*is & plene etat*is* qui *pre*sens in Cur*ia* vadiauit d*omi*no $ix^{s}iiij^{d}$ de Relevio suo & ffecit ffidelit*atem*

M*isericord*ia $vj^{s}iiij^{d}$ — Jtem *presentant* q*uo*d Joh*ann*a kellok ($viij^{d}$) Joh*ann*a Savegge ($viij^{d}$) Joh*ann*a Shott *serua* Joh*ann*is Broune ($viij^{d}$) ffreger*unt* Sepes apud Wodcott & ligna [1] inde asportauer*unt* ad ignem i*de*o rem*anent* in M*isericord*ia Et Joh*annes* yong (xij^{d}) succidit diu*ersos* Ramos vni*us* vlmi crescen*tis* in terr*a* d*omi*ni voc*ata* Curlys i*de*o ipse rem*anet* in M*isericord*ia Et henr*icus* hudson (xx^{d}) & Nich*ol*aus Wamer (xx^{d}) transiunt vlt*ra* terr*as* d*omi*ni cu*m* bigis suis diu*ersis* temp*or*ib*us* in p*re*iudic*ium* d*omi*ni i*de*o ipsi rem*anent* in M*isericord*ia p*ro*ut patet sup*er* eo*rum* Capit*a*

affur*atores* — Nich*ol*aus Waker, Will*elmus* legger — Jur*ati*

S*umma* hui*us* Cur*ie* $lxxij^{s}ij^{d}$

[1] MS: lingna

elief and of full age, who, present in court, paid 1520
9^s4^d to the lord 9^s4^d for his relief and did
ealty fealty.

nercement 6^s4^d Also, they present that Joan Kellok (8^d), Joan Savegge (8^d), Joan Shott, John Broune's servant (8^d), have broken down hedges at Woodcote and have carried away wood [1] thereof for firing. Therefore they remain in mercy. And John Yong (12^d) has cut various branches off an elm growing on land of the lord called Curlys. Therefore he remains in mercy. And Henry Hudson (20^d) and Nicholas Wamer (20^d) have encroached on the lord's lands with their carts at various times to the prejudice of the lord. Therefore they remain in mercy as appears above their heads.

Affeerers Nicholas Waker, William Legger Sworn

Amount of this court 72^s2^d

Bandon

Cur*ia* Nich*ol*ai Carew Milit*is* tent*a* ib*id*em xviij^{vo} die Marcij anno regni regis h*enrici* viij xij^{mo}

Esson*ium*

Null*um*

M*isericord*ia
xij^{d}

Homag*ium* ib*id*em videl*ic*et Thomas hunt Nich*ol*aus Waker Wille*lmu*s legger Simon Glover henr*icus* Shott Rob*er*tus Waker & Margareta lewes qui jur*ati* pr*esentant* qu*o*d alic*ia* Morley vidua Joh*ann*es Botery (iiij^{d}) Wille*lmu*s petley (iiij^{d}) & Tenen*s* terr*e* nup*er* [ ] May (iiij^{d}) sunt sect*atores* Cur*ie* & fac*iunt* def*altam* i*de*o ips*i* rem*anent* in M*isericord*ia p*ro*ut patet sup*er* eo*rum* Capit*a*

ffin*is*
vj^{d}

Ad hanc Cur*iam* ven*it* alic*ia* Morley vidua (vj^{d}) p*er* Alexandr*um* hunt Capellanu*m* & petit se admitti ad ffine*m* p*ro* sect*a* sua Cur*ie* hoc anno relaxand*a* cui conceditu*r* vt patet sup*er* eius Caput

alienacio

Jt*em* pr*esentant* qu*o*d Rob*er*tus Waker qui de do*mi*no tenuit lib*er*e vnu*m* ten*emen*tu*m* & cert*as* terr*as* cont*inentes* [ ] acr*as* terr*e* p*er* redditu*m* v^{s}ix^{d} p*er* annu*m* p*re*missa alienauit Joh*ann*i Waker ffr*atr*i suo qui p*re*sens in Cur*ia* cogn*ovit* teneri p*re*missa de do*mi*no p*er* redditu*m* p*re*d*ictu*m & fec*it* do*mi*no

ffidelit*as*

ffidel*itatem*

M*isericord*ia
xx^{d}

Jt*em* p*re*sent*ant* q*uo*d [ ] Colyn de Miccham vidua (xx^{d}) iniuste int*r*auit in vna

Bandon — A court of Nicholas Carew, knight, held there on the 18th day of March in the twelfth year of the reign of King Henry VIII. 1521

Essoin — None

Amercement 12^d — The homage there, namely: Thomas Hunt; Nicholas Waker; William Legger; Simon Glover; Henry Shott; Robert Waker and Margaret Lewes, who, being sworn, present that Alice Morley, widow, John Botery (4^d), William Petley (4^d) and the tenant of land late of [ ] May (4^d) are suitors at court and make default. Therefore they remain in mercy as appears above their heads.

Fine 6^d — To this court comes Alice Morley, widow (6^d), by Alexander Hunt, chaplain, and seeks to be admitted to a fine for her suit at court to be remitted this year and it is granted to her as appears above her head.

Alienation — Also, they present that Robert Waker, who held freely of the lord a tenement and certain lands containing [ ] acres of land at a rent of 5^s9^d a year, has alienated the premises to John Waker, his brother, who, present in court, has acknowledged that the premises are held of the lord for the rent

Fealty — aforementioned and has done fealty to the lord.

Amercement 20^d — Also they present that [ ] Colyn of Mitcham, widow (20^d), wrongfully entered

p*ar*cella terre de solo d*omi*ni voc*ato* Sundriche & ib*ide*m succidit diu*erso*s Ramos vni*us* quarci & eciam succidit diu*erso*s Spines & dumos in ead*e*m crescen*tes* ad p*re*iudic*iu*m d*omi*ni i*de*o ip*s*a rem*anet* in M*isericord*ia p*ro*ut patet sup*er* eius Caput

Extr*a*ct*a* delib*erata* Ballio

affur*atores* Thomas hunt / Rob*er*tus Waker Jur*ati*

S*umma* huiu*s* Cur*ie* iij[s]ij[d]

a parcel of land on land of the lord called 1521
Sundriche and there cut various branches off an oak and also cut down various thornbushes and brambles therein growing, to the prejudice of the lord. Therefore she remains in mercy as appears above her head.

Extract delivered to the bailiff.

Affeerers Thomas Hunt, Robert Waker Sworn

Amount of this court 3^s2^d

Bandon

Cur*ia* Nich*ol*ai Carew Milit*is* tent*a* ib*ide*m iij^{cio} die ap*ri*lis anno regni regis h*enrici* viij^{i} xiij^{mo}

Esson*ium*

Null*um*

M*isericord*ia xiiij^{d}

Homag*ium* ib*ide*m videl*ice*t Thomas hunt Nich*ol*aus Waker Will*elmu*s legger Joh*anne*s Waker Simon Glover & henr*icus* Shott qui Jur*ati* *presentant* qu*o*d Rob*er*tus Waker (iiij^{d}) Joh*anne*s Botery (iiij^{d}) Margareta lewys (ij^{d}) & tenen*s* terr*e* [ ] May (iiij^{d}) sunt sect*atores* Cur*ie* & fac*iunt* def*altam* *ideo* ip*s*i rem*anent* in M*isericord*ia

ffin*is* p*ro* secta Cur*ie* xij^{d}

Ad hanc Cur*iam* venerunt alic*ia* Morley vidua (vj^{d}) per Joh*anne*m Waker ffirmar*ium* suu*m* & Will*elmu*s petley (vj^{d}) pe*r* Joh*anne*m yong firmar*ium* suu*m* & petunt vt ip*s*i ad fine*m* p*ro* sect*a* sua Cur*ie* hoc anno respectuand*a* cui conceditu*r* p*ro*ut patet supe*r* eo*rum* Capita

M*isericord*ia viij^{s}viij^{d}

Jt*e*m p*resentant* qu*o*d Ric*ard*us Gylys (vj^{s}viij^{d}) & Thomas Webbe tenen*s* de Micch*a*m (ij^{s}) sup*e*ron*e*rant Com*muni*am de Bandon cu*m* ouib*us* suis cont*ra* cons*uetudinem* huiu*s* Man*e*rij & ad p*r*ejudic*ium* om*n*ium tenen*cium* ib*ide*m *ideo* ip*s*i rem*anent* in M*isericord*ia p*ro*ut patet supe*r* eo*rum* Capit*a*

Ext*r*act*a* delib*erata* ballio

affur*atores* Joh*anne*s Waker, Will*elmu*s legger Jur*ati*

S*umma* huiu*s* Cur*ie* x^{s}x^{d}

Bandon — A court of Nicholas Carew, knight, held there on the 3rd day of April in the thirteenth year of the reign of King Henry VIII. 1522

Essoin — None

Amercement 14^d — The homage there, namely: Thomas Hunt, Nicholas Waker, William Legger, John Waker, Simon Glover and Henry Shott, who, being sworn, present that Robert Waker (4^d), John Botery (4^d), Margaret Lewys (2^d) and the tenant of land of [ ] May (4^d) are suitors at court and make default. Therefore they remain in mercy.

Fine for suit at court 12^d — To this court came Alice Morley, widow (6^d), by John Waker her farmer, and William Petley (6^d), by John Yong his farmer, and seek that they *be admitted* to a fine for their suit at court this year to be respited. It is granted to them as appears above their heads.

Amercement 8^s8^d — Also, they present that Richard Gylys (6^s8^d) and Thomas Webbe, tenant of Mitcham (2^s), overload the common of Bandon with their sheep, against the custom of this manor and to the prejudice of all the tenants there. Therefore they remain in mercy as appears above their heads.

Extract delivered to the bailiff.

Affeerers John Waker, William Legger Sworn

Amount of this court 10^s10^d

Bandon

Cur*ia* Nich*ol*ai Carew Milit*is* tent*a* ib*ide*m die lune se*cun*do Marcij anno regni Regis henrici Octaui quartodecimo

Esson*ium*

Null*um*

M*isericord*ia ij^{s}

Homagiu*m* ib*ide*m videl*ice*t Thomas hunt Rob*er*tus Waker Joh*ann*es Waker Will*elmu*s legger Simon Glover & henricus Shott qui Jur*ati* p*r*esent*ant* q*uo*d Joh*ann*es Botery (vj^{d}) Tenen*s* terr*e* Will*elm*i May (vj^{d}) Tenen*s* terr*e* nup*er* alic*ie* Morley vidue (vj^{d}) & Will*elmu*s petley (vj^{d}) sunt sect*atores* Cur*ie* & fac*iunt* def*altam* i*de*o ip*s*i rem*anent* in M*isericord*ia p*r*out patet sup*er* eo*rum* Capit*a*

Distr*ingere*

Jte*m* p*r*esent*ant* q*uo*d alic*ia* Morley vidua qui de d*omi*no tenuit lib*e*re cert*as* terr*as* & Ten*emen*ta videl*ice*t vnu*m* Ten*emen*tu*m* & cert*am* terr*am* voc*atam* Wanellys p*er* redditu*m* ij^{s}iiij^{d} p*er* annu*m* vnu*m* Ten*emen*tu*m* & cert*am* terr*am* voc*atam* doggys p*er* redditu*m* x^{s} p*er* annu*m* vnu*m* ten*emen*tu*m* & cert*am* terra*m* voc*atam* heys p*er* redditu*m* xvj^{d} p*er* annu*m* ac vnu*m* ten*emen*tu*m* nup*er* Will*elm*i lithier & quondam Donnyng*is* p*er* reddit*um* iiij^{s} p*er* annu*m* obijt inde sei*sita* & q*uo*d Dorothia ux*or* Will*elm*i Wylde est Consanguinia & heres d*ict*e alicie & plene etatis videl*ice*t ffilia Joh*an*ne ffilie d*ict*e alicie quem quide*m* Will*elmu*m Wylde p*re*ceptu*m* est Ballio distr*ingere* p*ro* xvij^{s}viij^{d} de Relevio ac p*ro* h*er*iett*o* & ffidelit*ate* d*omi*no debit*is* p*er* morte*m* d*ict*e alicie citr*a* p*ro*x*imam* Cur*iam*

Ext*r*act*a* delib*erata* ballio

Bandon A court of Nicholas Carew, knight, held there on Monday the 2nd of March in the fourteenth year of the reign of King Henry VIII. 1523

Essoin None

Amercement 2^s The homage there, namely: Thomas Hunt, Robert Waker, John Waker, William Legger, Simon Glover and Henry Shott, who, being sworn, present that John Botery (6^d), the tenant of land of William May (6^d), the tenant of land late of Alice Morley widow (6^d), and William Petley (6^d) are suitors at court and make default. Therefore they remain in mercy as appears above their heads.

Distrain Also, they present that Alice Morley, widow, who held freely of the lord certain lands and tenements, namely: a tenement and certain land called Wanellys for a rent of 2^s4^d a year; a tenement and certain land called Doggys for a rent of 10^s a year; a tenement and certain land called Heys for a rent of 16^d a year, and a tenement, late of William Lithier and formerly Donnyng's, for a rent of 4^s a year, has died seised thereof; and that Dorothy, wife of William Wylde, is kinswoman and heir of the said Alice, namely the daughter of Joan, daughter of the said Alice, and of full age. And the order is given to the bailiff to distrain the said William Wylde for 17^s8^d as relief and for the heriot and fealty due to the lord through the death of the said Alice before the next court.

Extract delivered to the bailiff

affur*atum* pe*r* homagiu*m* tunc p*re*sens

S*umma* hui*us* Cur*ie* ij[s]

Affeered by the homage then present 1523

Amount of this court 2^{s}

Bandon — Cur*i*a Nich*o*l*a*i Carew Milit*i*s tent*a* ib*i*d*e*m vltim*o* die ffebruarij anno regni Regis henrici Octaui quintodecimo

Esson*ium* — Null*um*

distr*ingere* — adhuc p*re*ceptu*m* est distr*ingere* tenen*tem* terr*e* Wille*lm*i Wylde in cert*a* terr*a* nup*er* alicie Morley p*ro* h*e*riett*o* et xvij^{s}viij^{d} de Relevio d*om*ino acceden*ti* p*er* mortem dict*e* alicie citra p*roxi*m*am* Cur*i*a*m*

M*isericord*ia xxij^{d} — Homagiu*m* ib*i*d*e*m videl*ic*et Thomas hunt Rob*er*tus Waker Joh*anne*s Waker Wille*lmus* legger Simon Glover Henr*icus* Shott Joh*anne*s Shornford Jure vx*or*is sue qui Jur*ati* p*re*sent*ant* qu*o*d Wille*lmu*s Wylde (vj^{d}) Jure ux*or*is sue Joh*anne*s Botery (vj^{d}) Nich*o*l*a*us Waker (ij^{d}) Wille*lmu*s May (iiij^{d}) Wille*lmu*s petley (iiij^{d}) sunt sect*atores* Cur*ie* et fac*iunt* def*altam* J*de*o rem*anent* in M*isericord*ia quilibet eo*rum* p*ro*ut patet sup*er* eius Capud

M*isericord*ia iiij^{s}iiij^{d} — Jtem p*re*sent*ant* qu*o*d Ric*ard*us Wryght de Carsalton (xl^{d}) iniuste occupat Co*mmun*iam ib*i*d*e*m voc*atam* Bedyngton heth cum anim*ali*js suis in p*re*iudic*ium* d*omi*ni et tenen*cium* Et qu*o*d Joh*anne*s Stapyll ffirmar*ius* Man*er*ij ib*i*d*e*m (xij^{d}) sup*e*ron*e*rat Co*mmun*iam p*re*dict*am* cu*m* ouibus suis J*de*o rem*anent* in M*isericord*ia quilibet eo*rum* p*ro*ut patet & *cetera*

Ext*r*act*a* delib*erata* Ballio

Bandon — A court of Nicholas Carew, knight, held there on the last day (29th) of February in the fifteenth year of the reign of King Henry VIII. 1524

Essoin — None

Distrain — At this time the order is given to distrain the tenant of land of William Wylde on certain land late of Alice Morley for a heriot and 17^{s} 8^{d} for relief falling due to the lord through the death of the said Alice before the next court.

Amercement 22^{d} — The homage there, namely: Thomas Hunt, Robert Waker, John Waker, William Legger, Simon Glover, Henry Shott, John Shornford in right of his wife, who, being sworn, present that William Wylde (6^{d}) in right of his wife, John Botery (6^{d}), Nicholas Waker (2^{d}), William May (4^{d}), William Petley (4^{d}) are suitors at court and make default. Therefore they remain in mercy, each and every one of them as appears above his head.

Amercement $4^{s}4^{d}$ — Also, they present that Richard Wryght of Carshalton (40^{d}) wrongfully occupies the common there, called Beddington Heath, with his beasts to the prejudice of the lord and the tenants; and that John Stapyll, farmer of the manor there (12^{d}), overloads the aforementioned common with his sheep. Therefore they remain in mercy, each one of them as appears etc..

Extract delivered to the bailiff

affur*atores*	Rob*er*tus Waker Will*elmu*s legger	Jur*ati*

S*um*m*a* hui*us* Cur*ie* vj^{s}ij^{d}

Affeerers	Robert Waker William Legger	Sworn	1524

Amount of this court 6^s2^d

Bandon | Curia Nicholai Carew Militis tenta ibidem xxvij^{o} die Marcij anno regni Regis henrici octaui sextodecimo

Essonium | Nullum

Distringere | adhuc preceptum est distringere Tenentem terre Willelmi Wylde in certis terris nuper alicie Morley pro herietto & xvij^{s}viij^{d} de Relevio domino accidenti per mortem dicte alicie citra proximam Curiam

Misericordia x^{d} | Homagium ibidem videlicet Johannes Botery Thomas hunt Johannes Waker Willelmus legger Simon Glover henricus Shott & Johannes Shornford Jure uxoris qui Jurati presentant quod Willelmus Wylde (vj^{d}) Jure uxoris Willelmus Maij (iiij^{d}) & Willelmus petley (iiij^{d}) sunt sectatores Curie & ffaciunt defaltam ideo ipsi remanent in Misericordia prout patet super eorum Capita

obitus | Jtem presentant quod Nicholaus Waker qui de domino tenuit libere [ ] per redditum vj^{s}iij^{d} obijt post vltimam Curiam per cuius mortem nihil accidit domino de herietto quia nullum habuit animall Et quod ipse ante mortem suam inde feoffauit Thomam hunt & alios Et quod Johannes Waker est eius ffilius & heres & plene etatis qui presens in Curia cognovit tenere premissa de

Relevium vj^{s}iij^{d} | domino per redditum predictum Et vadiauit vj^{s}iij^{d} de Relevio suo domino accidenti per

Bandon	A court of Nicholas Carew, knight, held there on the 27th day of March in the sixteenth year of the reign of King Henry VIII.	1525
Essoin	None	
Distrain	At this time the order is given to distrain before the next court the tenant of land of William Wylde in certain lands, late of Alice Morley, for heriot and 17^s8^d as relief falling due to the lord through the death of the said Alice.	
Amercement 10^d	The homage there, namely: John Botery, Thomas Hunt, John Waker, William Legger, Simon Glover, Henry Shott and John Shornford in right of his wife, who, being sworn, present that William Wylde (6^d) in right of his wife, William May (4^d) and William Petley (4^d) are suitors at court and make default. Therefore they remain in mercy as appears above their heads.	
Death Relief 6^s3^d	Also, they present that Nicholas Waker, who held freely of the lord [ ] for a rent of 6^s3^d, died after the last court, by whose death nothing fell to the lord as heriot because he had no beast. And that he, before his death, therein feoffed Thomas Hunt and others. And that John Waker is his son and heir and of full age, who, present in court, acknowledged that he holds the premises of the lord for the aforementioned rent. And he paid 6^s3^d as his relief, falling	

mort*em* d*i*c*t*i Nich*o*l*a*i Et fecit

ffidelit*as* ffidelit*atem* & *cetera*

alienaci*o* Jt*e*m p*resentant* q*uo*d Rob*er*tus Waker qui de d*omi*no tenuit libere vnu*m* Ten*emen*tum & vnu*m* gardinu*m* & d*imidiam* virgat*am* terr*e* nup*er* Wille*l*m*i* Mokell p*er* reddit*um* xx^{d} & octo acr*as* terr*e* nup*er* Thome holden p*er* reddit*um* xij^{d} vnu*m* ten*emen*tum d*i*c*t*i Thome holden p*er* reddit*um* xviij^{d} ac vna*m* acr*am* terr*e* & d*imidiam* nup*er* Rob*er*ti Wannell p*er* reddit*um* ij^{d} obijt post vlti*m*am Cur*iam* Et q*uo*d ipse ante morte*m* sua*m* p*re*missa vendidit cuid*a*m Joh*anni* hyller qui quid*e*m Joh*anne*s h*ab*et diem

Dies vs*que* pr*o*x*imam* Cur*iam* ostend*ere* eviden*ciam* inde

M*i*s*e*r*i*c*o*r*d*ia x^{s} Jt*e*m p*resentant* q*uo*d Joh*anne*s Stapyll ffirmar*ius* d*omi*ni (xx^{d}) succidit & amputauit diu*ers*a*s* arbores & diu*ers*o*s* ramos arboru*m* in terris d*omi*ni p*ar*cell*a* ffirme sue i*de*o rem*anet* in M*i*s*e*r*i*c*o*r*d*ia Et q*uo*d Rob*er*tus Walker (xx^{d}) s*i*milit*er* amputauit & succid*i*t diu*ers*a*s* arbores in le bornfeld Et Joh*anne*s Skete (xx^{d}) sim*i*lit*er* amputauit & succidit diu*ers*a*s* arbores & Ramos arboru*m* apud le Sandhyll Et Ric*ar*dus Wryght (xx^{d}) s*i*milit*er* amputauit & succid*i*t diu*ers*a*s* arbores & Ramos diu*ersarum* arbo*rum* in terr*a* d*omi*ni voc*ata* Godfreyes Et ide*m* Ric*ar*dus (iij^{s}iiij^{d}) iniuste occupat Com*mun*iam cu*m* ouib*us* & alijs an*i*m*a*l*i*js suis contr*a* consuet*udinem* hui*us* Man*eri*j i*de*o ipsi rem*anent* in M*i*s*e*r*i*c*o*r*d*ia

Dies Adhuc om*n*es tenen*tes* hui*us* d*omi*nij h*ab*ent die*m*
pene Justificand*os* porcos suos citr*a* Cl*ause*um pasche

due to the lord through the death of the said Nicholas. And he did fealty etc.. 1525

Fealty

Alienation

Also, they present that Robert Waker, who held freely of the lord a tenement and a garden and half a virgate of land, late of William Mokell, for a rent of 20^d; and eight acres of land, late of Thomas Holden, for a rent of 12^d; a tenement of the said Thomas Holden for a rent of 18^d, and an acre and a half of land, late of Robert Wannell, for a rent of 2^d, died after the last court. And that he, before his death, sold the premises to a certain John Hyller and the same John has a day before the next court to show the evidence thereof.

Day

Amercement 10^s

Also, they present that John Stapyll, the lord's farmer (20^d), has cut down and cut off various trees and various branches of trees on the lord's lands *on* a parcel of his farm, therefore he remains in mercy: and that Robert Walker (20^d) likewise cut off and cut down various trees in le Bourn Field: and John Skete (20^d) likewise cut off and cut down various trees and branches of trees at le Sand Hill: and Richard Wryght (20^d) likewise cut off and cut down various trees and branches of various trees on land of the lord called Godfreyes: and the same Richard ($3^s 4^d$) wrongfully occupies the common with his sheep and other animals against the custom of this manor. Therefore they remain in mercy.

Penalty day

At this time all the tenants of this lordship have a day for the licensing of their pigs

p*ro*x*ime* futur*e* quili*be*t eo*rum* sub pena p*ro* quoli*be*t porco iiij[d]

affur*atores*	Thomas hunt Simon Glover	Jur*ati*

Ext*r*act*a* delib*erata* Ballio

S*um*m*a* hui*us* Cur*ie* xvij[s]j[d]

before the Close of Easter next to come (23rd April), each and every one of them under a penalty for each and every pig of 4d. 1525

Affeerers Thomas Hunt, Simon Glover Sworn

Extract delivered to the bailiff

Amount of this court 17s1d

Bandon — Cur*ia* Nich*ol*ai Carew Milit*is* tent*a* ib*id*em penultim*o* die ffebruarij anno regni Regis henrici Octaui decimo septim*o*

Esson*ium* — Null*um*

dies — Adhuc Joh*ann*es hyller h*ab*et diem ult*er*iorem ostendend*am* eviden*ciam* cert*is* terr*is* nup*er* p*er* ipsum empt*is* de Rob*er*to Waker citr*a* p*roxim*am Cur*iam*

vadiac*io* Relevij — Ad hanc Cur*iam* Ballius ven*it* & cogn*ovit* se esse satisfact*um* & solut*um* de xvij^{s}vij^{d} ob*olo* de Relevio Dorathie vx*or*is Wille*lm*i Whylde Consanguini*e* & her*edis* alicie Morley d*omi*no accident*i* p*er* mortem d*ict*e alicie   i*de*o cess*it* p*ro*cess*us*

M*isericord*ia ij^{s} — Homagiu*m* ib*id*em videl*ic*et Joh*ann*es Botery Thomas hunt Joh*ann*es Waker Wille*lmus* legger & henr*icus* Shott qui Jur*ati* p*resentant* qu*o*d Wille*lmus* Wylde (vj^{d}) Jure vx*or*is Wille*lmus* May (iiij^{d}) Wille*lmus* petley (iiij^{d}) Joh*ann*es hiller (iiij^{d}) Margareta Shernford (ij^{d}) Joh*ann*es Waker de Carsalton (ij^{d}) & Simon Glover (ij^{d}) [1] sunt sect*atores* Cur*ie* & ffac*iunt* def*altam*   i*de*o ipsi rem*anent* in m*isericord*ia

M*isericord*ia vj^{d} — Jtem p*resentant* qu*o*d Joh*ann*es yong (ij^{d}) iniuste succidit diu*ersos* dumos crescent*es* in terr*a* d*omi*ni iacent*i* iux*ta* terr*am* Joh*ann*is Waker in Waddon Marke   i*de*o rem*anet* in

[1] qui cancelled.

Bandon A court of Nicholas Carew, knight, held there on the penultimate day (27th) of February in the seventeenth year of the reign of King Henry VIII. 1526

Essoin None

Day At this time John Hyller has a further day, before the next court, to show evidence concerning certain lands lately bought by him from Robert Waker.

Payment of relief To this court came the bailiff and acknowledged that he was satisfied, having been paid the $17^s 7\frac{1}{2}^d$ relief of Dorothy, kinswoman and heir of Alice Morley and wife of William Whylde, which fell due to the lord by the death of the said Alice. Therefore the lawsuit has ceased.

Amercement 2^s The homage there, namely: John Botery, Thomas Hunt, John Waker, William Legger and Henry Shott, who, being sworn, present that William Wylde (6^d) in right of his wife; William May (4^d); William Petley (4^d); John Hiller (4^d); Margaret Shernford (2^d); John Waker of Carshalton (2^d) and Simon Glover (2^d) [1] are suitors at court and make default. Therefore they remain in mercy.

Amercement 6^d Also, they present that John Yong (2^d) wrongfully cut down various thornbushes growing on land of the lord lying next to land of John Waker in Waddon Mark. Therefore he remains in

Misericordia prout patet Et *quod* idem Johannes yong (ij^{d}) & Johannes Waker de Carsalton (ij^{d}) *permittunt* porcos suos *pertransire* iniustific*atos* contra ordinac*ionem* inde fact*am* *ideo* rem*anent* in *Misericordia*

Ordinac*io* Ad hanc Cur*iam* ordinat*um* est tam p*er* auctoritate*m* hui*us* Cur*ie* qu*am* p*er* assens*um* om*nium* tenen*cium* qu*od* omnes tenen*tes* h*ab*ent*es* aliquas [1] oues infra istud d*ominium* decetero non custod*iant* aliquas [1] oues in Co*mmun*ia voc*ata* le heth inter festu*m* s*an*cti Georgij & festu*m* s*an*cti Mich*aelis* arch*angeli* sub p*ena* quili*be*t eo*rum* x^{s}

affur*atores* Johannes Botery / Wille*lmus* legger Jur*ati*

Ext*ra*ct*a* delib*erata* Ballio

S*umma* hui*us* Cur*ie* xx^{s}j^{d} obol*us*

[1] MS: aliquos.

mercy as appears; and that the same John Yong (2^d) and John Waker of Carshalton (2^d) allow their pigs to wander unlicensed against the order made thereon. Therefore they remain in mercy. 1526

Order

At this court it is ordered, both by the authority of this court and with the assent of all the tenants, that all tenants who have any [1] sheep within this lordship shall not henceforth keep any [2] sheep on the common called le Heath between the feast of Saint George (23rd April) and the feast of Saint Michael the Archangel (29th September), under penalty, for each and every one of them, of 10^s.

Affeerers John Botery, William Legger Sworn

Extract delivered to the bailiff

Amount of this court $20^s 1\frac{1}{2}^d$

Bandon	Cur*ia* Nich*ol*ai Carew Milit*is* tent*a* ib*idem* xviij° die Marcij anno regni Regis henrici octaui decimo octauo
Esson*ium*	Null*um*
M*isericord*ia xviij^{d}	Homagi*um* ib*idem* videl*icet* Joh*ann*es Botery Thomas hunt Joh*ann*es hyller Joh*ann*es Waker Simon Glover & Will*elmu*s legger qui Jur*ati* pr*esent*ant quod Will*elmu*s Wylde (vj^{d}) Jure vx*or*is Will*elmu*s May (iiij^{d}) Will*elmu*s petley (iiij^{d}) & Margareta Shernford (iiij^{d}) sunt sect*atores* Cur*ie* & fac*iunt* def*altam* i*de*o ipsi rem*anent* in M*isericord*ia p*ro*ut patet sup*er* eo*rum* Capita
alienacio	Jt*em* p*resentant* q*uo*d Joh*ann*es Waker de Carsalton qui de d*omi*no libere vnu*m* Ten*emen*tu*m* & cert*am* terr*am* cont*inentem* circa xj acr*as* terre vocat*am* [ ] p*er* reddit*um* [ ] p*er* annu*m* p*re*missa vendidit Ric*ard*o Knep de Miccham qui p*re*sens in Cur*ia* cogn*ovit* tenere p*re*missa de d*omi*no p*er* p*redictum* Reddit*um* & fecit d*omi*no ffidelit*atem*
ffidelit*as*	
obitus	Jt*em* p*resentant* q*uo*d henr*icus* [1] Shott qui de d*omi*no tenuit libere Jure Joh*anne* [2] vx*or*is sue vnu*m* ten*emen*tu*m* cu*m* gardino adiacen*ti* voc*atum* [ ] p*er* reddit*um* xx^{d} p*er* annu*m* obijt ipsaq*ue* Joh*ann*a [3] ip*sum* sup*er*uixit

[1] Joh*ann*es cancelled.
[2] Alic*ie* cancelled
[3] alicia cancelled

Bandon

A court of Nicholas Carew, knight, held there on the 18th day of March in the eighteenth year of the reign of King Henry VIII. 1527

Essoin

None

Amercement 18^d

The homage there, namely: John Botery, Thomas Hunt, John Hyller, John Waker, Simon Glover and William Legger, who, being sworn, present that William Wylde (6^d) in right of his wife, William May (4^d), William Petley (4^d) and Margaret Shernford (4^d) are suitors at court and make default. Therefore they remain in mercy as appears above their heads.

Alienation

Also, they present that John Waker of Carshalton, who *held* freely of the lord a tenement and certain land containing about eleven acres of land, called [ ], at a rent of [ ] a year, has sold the premises to Richard Knep of Mitcham who, present in court, acknowledged that he holds the premises of the

Fealty

lord at the aforementioned rent and did fealty to the lord.

Death

Also, they present that Henry [1] Shott, who held freely of the lord in right of Joan [2] his wife a tenement with a garden adjacent called [ ] at a rent of 20^d a year, has died and the same Joan [3] has

& nupta est cuidam Joh*anni* Rydley qui *pre*sens in Cur*ia* cogn*ovit* tener*e* *pre*missa vt in Jure ipsius Joh*an*ne & fecit ffidelit*atem*

ffidelit*as*

M*isericord*ia xij^{d} — Jtem *pre*s*entant* qu*o*d Ric*ardus* [1] Gylis de Miccham (xij^{d}) sup*er*on*er*at Commu*n*iam ib*idem* voc*atam* le heth cum anim*ali*js suis i*deo* ip*s*e rem*anet* in M*isericord*ia pr*o*ut patet sup*er* eius Caput Et h*ab*et die*m* neampleus sic faciendu*m* sub p*ena* vj^{s}viij^{d}

Dies — Adhuc Joh*ann*es hiller h*ab*et die*m* vlt*er*iorem ostendend*am* euidenc*iam* quomodo tenet cert*am* terr*am* nup*er* Rob*er*t*i* Waker citr*a* p*roximam* Cur*iam*

Ordinac*io* sub p*ena* — Ad hanc Cur*iam* ordinatu*m* est tam p*er* assensu*m* omn*i*um tenen*ci*um qu*a*m auctoritate hui*us* Cur*ie* qu*o*d omnes tenent*es* siue inh*a*bitant*es* infra istud d*omini*um h*a*bente*s* aliquos porcos vlt*ra* festu*m* annunc*iacionis* be*ate* Marie [2] quolibe*t* anno non p*er*mittunt eos p*er*transire iniustificat*os* sub p*ena* p*ro* quolibe*t* porco ij^{d}

affur*atores*	Thomas hunt Joh*ann*es Hiller	Jur*ati*

Ext*racta* deli*berata* Ballio

S*umma* hui*us* Cur*ie* ij^{s}vj^{d}

1 Joh*ann*es cancelled.

2 non cancelled

survived him and has married a certain John Rydley who, present in court, acknowledged that he holds the premises as in right of the same Joan and did fealty. 1527

ealty

mercement 12^d

Also, they present that Richard[1] Gylis of Mitcham (12^d) overloads the common at that place called le Heath with his beasts. Therefore he remains in mercy as appears above his head and has a day by which no longer to do so, under a penalty of 6^s8^d.

ay

At this time John Hiller has a further day, before the next court, to show evidence of how he holds certain land late of Robert Waker.

rder under enalty

At this court it is ordered, both with the assent of all the tenants and by the authority of this court, that all tenants or inhabitants within this lordship who have any pigs shall not allow then to wander unlicensed after the feast of the Annunciation of the blessed Mary (25th March)[2] in any year, under a penalty for each and every pig of 2^d.

Affeerers Thomas Hunt, John Hiller Sworn

Extract delivered to the bailiff

Amount of this court 2^s6^d

Bandon — Cur*ia* Nich*ol*ai Carew Milit*is* tent*a* ib*id*em quarto die Marcij anno regni Regis henrici octaui decimo nono

Essoni*um* — Null*um*

Dies — Adhuc dies dat*us* est Joh*ann*i hiller vsq*ue* p*ro*x*im*am Cur*iam* ad ostendend*am* evidenc*iam* quomodo tenet cert*as* terr*as* nup*er* p*er* ips*um* empt*as* [1] de Rob*er*to Waker

M*isericord*ia ij^{s} — Homagi*um* ib*id*em videl*icet* Joh*ann*es Botery Joh*ann*es hiller Joh*ann*es Waker Will*elmu*s legger & Joh*ann*es Rydley qui Jur*ati* p*resentant* quod Will*elmu*s Wylde (vj^{d}) Jure vx*or*is Thomas hunt (p*er*cep*tum*) Will*elmu*s May (iiij^{d}) Will*elmu*s petley (iiij^{d}) Ricardus Knep (iiij^{d}) Margareta Shernford (ij^{d}) & Simon Glover (iiij^{d}) sunt sect*atores* Cur*ie* & ffac*iunt* def*altam* i*deo* ip*si* rem*anent* in M*isericord*ia

p*ena* for*is* iij^{s}iiij^{d} — Jt*em* p*resentant* q*uo*d Joh*ann*es Richebell de Walyngton ffirmar*ius* d*omi*ni (iij^{s}iiij^{d}) ib*id*em iniuste & cont*ra* ordinac*io*nem inde p*ri*us fact*am* occupat Commu*ni*am voc*atam* le heth inter festu*m* s*anc*ti Georg*ii* & ffestu*m* s*anc*ti Mich*ael*is i*deo* incurr*it* pena*m* inde tamen moderat*am* p*er* tenenc*iam* vt patet

M*isericord*ia xj^{s}viiij^{d} — & q*uo*d Ric*ard*us Wryght (iij^{s}iiij^{d}) sup*er*on*er*at Commu*ni*am p*redi*ct*am* cu*m* anim*ali*js suis cont*ra*

[1] p*er* cancelled.

andon — A court of Nicholas Carew, knight, held there on the 4th day of March in the nineteenth year of the reign of King Henry VIII. 1528

ssoin — None

ay — At this time a day is given to John Hiller, before the next court, to show evidence of his right to hold certain lands lately bought [1] by him from Robert Waker.

mercement 2s — The homage there, namely: John Botery, John Hiller, John Waker, William Legger and John Rydley, who, being sworn, present that William Wylde (6d) in right of his wife, Thomas Hunt (received), William May (4d), William Petley (4d), Richard Knep (4d), Margaret Shernford (2d) and Simon Glover (4d) are suitors at court and make default. Therefore they remain in mercy.

enalty for utdoor ffences 3s 4d — Also, they present that John Richebell of Wallington, farmer of the lord there (3s 4d), wrongfully and against the order earlier made thereon, occupies the common called le Heath between the feast of Saint George (23rd April) and the feast of Saint Michael (29th September). Therefore he incurs the penalty, moderated, however, through his tenancy, as appears.

mercement 11s 8d — And that Richard Wryght (3s 4d) overloads the aforementioned common with his beasts against cons*uetudinem* hui*us* Man*er*ij Et Ric*ard*us Gylis (iij^{s}iiij^{d}) Thomas Webbe (xx^{d}) & Thomas fforman (iij^{s}iiij^{d}) Tenent*es* de Miccham sup*er*oner*ant* Co*mmuni*am cu*m* ani*malij*s suis *ideo* ipsi rem*anent* in M*isericord*ia p*r*out patet sup*er* eo*rum* Capit*a*

pena for*is* xx^{d} Cu*m* ad vltimam Cur*iam* ordinat*um* fuit q*uo*d om*n*es inh*ab*itant*es* hui*us* d*omi*nij quolib*et* anno cit*ra* festu*m* annunc*iacionis* be*ate* Marie iustific*arent* porcos suos sub pena p*ro* quolib*et* porco ij^{d} quid*am* tamen Joh*ann*es yong (xij^{d}) cu*m* xv porc*is* Joh*ann*es Whatman (iiij^{d}) cu*m* x porc*is* Ric*ard*us Glover (vj^{d}) cu*m* xjj porc*is* ordinac*i*on*em* p*redictam* ffreger*unt* in p*er*mittend*o* porcos suos p*redic*tos p*er*transire iniustific*atos* *ideo* incurr*erunt* pena*m* p*r*out patet sup*er* eo*rum* Capit*a*

M*isericord*ia xx^{d} Jtem p*resentant* q*uo*d Wille*lmu*s hardys ffirmar*ius* Wille*lm*i Wylde ac ffirmar*ius* d*omi*ni (xx^{d}) p*r*ostrauit una*m* vlmu*m* crescen*tem* in vna p*ar*cella terr*e* cont*inenti* circiter d*imidiam* acr*am* terr*e* iacen*tem* ex p*ar*te australi orrei p*redicti* Wille*lm*i Wylde *ideo* rem*anet* in M*isericord*ia

affur*atores* Joh*ann*es Waker, Wille*lmu*s legger Jur*ati*

Ext*r*act*a* delib*erata* Ballio

S*umma* hui*us* Cur*ie* xx^{s}iiij^{d}

the custom of this manor; and Richard Gylis (3^{s}4^{d}), Thomas Webbe (20^{d}) and Thomas Forman (3^{s}4^{d}), tenants of Mitcham, overload the common with their beasts. Therefore they remain in mercy as appears above their heads. 1528

enalty for utdoor ffences 20^{d}

Although at the last court it was ordered that all the inhabitants of this lordship should license their pigs every year before the feast of the Annunciation of the blessed Mary (25th March) under penalty for each and every pig of 2^{d}, nevertheless a certain John Yong (12^{d}) with fifteen pigs, John Whatman (4^{d}) with ten pigs, Richard Glover (6^{d}) with twelve pigs, have broken the aforementioned order in allowing their pigs aforesaid to wander unlicensed. Therefore they have incurred the penalty as appears above their heads.

nercement 20^{d}

Also, they present that William Hardys, farmer of William Wylde and farmer of the lord (20^{d}), cut down an elm growing on a parcel of land containing about half an acre of land lying on the southern side of a barn of the aforementioned William Wylde. Therefore he remains in mercy.

Affeerers John Waker William Legger Sworn

Extract delivered to the bailiff

Amount of this court 20^{s}4^{d}

Bedyngton Cur*ia* Nich*ol*ai Carew Milit*is* tent*a* ib*ide*m quarto die Marcij anno regni Regis henrici octaui decimonono

Esson*ium* Null*um*

M*isericord*ia xij^{d} Homagiu*m* ib*ide*m videl*ice*t Thomas hewett petrus Bonewyke Henr*icus* Staplerst & Thomas hunt qui Jur*ati* p*re*sent*ant* q*uo*d prior de Reygate (iiij^{d}) Joh*ann*es Codyngton de Codyngton (iiij^{d}) Joh*ann*es Skynner (iiij^{d}) sunt sect*atores* Cur*ie* & fac*iunt* def*altam* i*de*o ipsi rem*anent* *in* M*isericord*ia p*ro*ut patet sup*er* eo*rum* Capit*a*

Alienac*io* Jt*em* p*resentant* q*uo*d Joh*ann*es Bristow de logge qui de d*omi*no tenuit lib*e*re cert*am* terr*am* voc*atam* lakelond in horley quond*am* Bornes p*er* reddit*um* v^{s}iij^{d} p*er* annu*m* p*re*missa ante mortem suam vendidit & dedit petro Bonewyke qui p*re*sens in Cur*ia* cogn*ovit* teneri p*re*missa de d*omi*no p*er* reddit*um* p*re*d*ictum* Et fecit d*omi*no

ffidelit*as* ffidelit*atem* & *cetera*

Alien*acio* Jt*em* p*re*sent*ant* q*uo*d Joh*ann*es pope qui de d*omi*no tenuit lib*e*re vnam p*ar*cell*am* terre iac*entem* in horley voc*atam* Chapmans p*er* reddit*um* iij^{s}iiij^{d} p*er* annu*m* p*re*missa vendidit Joh*anni* Caryll quiquidem Joh*ann*es Caryll eandem vendid*it* Jacobo Skynner de Reygate qui cogn*ovit* tener*e* p*re*missa de d*omi*no Et ffecit

ffidelit*as* ffidelit*atem*

affur*atum* p*er* homagiu*m* tunc p*resens*

S*umma* huiu*s* Cur*ie* xij^{d}

Beddington

A court of Nicholas Carew, knight, held there on the 4th day of March in the nineteenth year of the reign of King Henry VIII. 1528

Essoin

None

Amercement 12^{d}

The homage there, namely: Thomas Hewett, Peter Bonewyke, Henry Staplerst and Thomas Hunt, who, being sworn, present that the prior of Reigate (4^{d}), John Codyngton of Codyngton (4^{d}), John Skynner (4^{d}) are suitors at court and make default. Therefore they remain in mercy as appears above their heads.

Alienation

Also, they present that John Bristow of Logge, who held freely of the lord a certain land, called Lakeland, in Horley, late Borne's, at a rent of $5^{s}3^{d}$ a year, sold the premises before his death and gave *them* to Peter Bonewyke who, present in court, acknowledged that the premises are held of the lord for the aforementioned rent.

Fealty

And he did fealty to the lord etc..

Alienation

Also, they present that John Pope, who held freely of the lord a parcel of land lying in Horley, called Chapmans, for a rent of $3^{s}4^{d}$ a year, has sold the premises to John Caryll, and the same John Caryll sold the same *premises* to Jacob Skynner of Reigate, who acknowledged that he holds the premises of the lord. And

Fealty

he did fealty.

Affeered by the homage then present

Amount of this court 12^{d}

Bandon	Cur*ia* Nich*ol*ai Carew Milit*is* tent*a* ib*idem* xxiij die ffebruarij anno regni Regis henrici Octaui vicesimo
Esson*ium*	Null*um*
Distr*ingere*	Cu*m* ad vlti*m*am Cur*iam* dies dat*us* fuit Joh*anni* hiller vs*que* hanc Cur*iam* ad ostend*endam* euidenc*iam* quomodo tenet cert*am* terr*am* nup*er* Rob*er*ti Waker & non ven*it* i*de*o pr*e*cep*tum* est Ballio ib*idem* q*uo*d distr*ingat* eund*e*m Joh*ann*em Jta q*uo*d sit ad p*roxim*am Cur*iam* ad ostend*endum* quomodo pr*e*missa tenet
M*isericord*ia xvj^{d}	Homagiu*m* ib*ide*m videl*ice*t Joh*ann*es Botery Thomas hunt Joh*ann*es hiller Joh*ann*es Waker Wille*lmu*s legger & Joh*ann*es Rydley Jure vx*or*is qui Jur*ati* p*resentant* q*uo*d Wille*lmu*s Wylde (viij^{d}) Jur*e* vx*or*is Wille*lmu*s May (ij^{d}) Ric*ar*dus knep (iiij^{d}) & Simon Glover (ij^{d}) sunt sect*atores* Cur*ie* & fac*iunt* def*altam* i*de*o ipsi rem*anent* in M*isericord*ia p*ro*ut patet sup*er* eo*rum* Capit*a*
Obitus Dies	Jt*e*m p*resentant* q*uo*d Wille*lmu*s petley qui de d*omi*no tenuit libere vnu*m* ten*ementum* & cert*am* terr*am* voc*atam* Ballis p*er* reddit*um* ij^{s}iij^{d} obijt post vlti*m*am Cur*iam* vt*e*rinu*s* ali*cui* vel non adhuc ignorant Et quis est eius p*roximus* here*s* adhuc s*imi*lit*er* ignorant Et i*de*o h*ab*ent die*m* vsq*ue* p*roxim*am Cur*iam* melius inde inquirend*um*
M*isericord*ia xx^{d}	Jt*e*m p*resentant* q*uo*d Ric*ar*dus Gylis de Miccham (xx^{d}) sup*e*ron*e*rat Co*mmun*iam voc*atam* le heth

Bandon A court of Nicholas Carew, knight, held there on the 23rd day of February in the twentieth year of the reign of King Henry VIII. 1529

Essoin None

Distrain Whereas at the last court a day was given to John Hiller before this court to show evidence of how he holds certain land late of Robert Waker, and he did not come, therefore the order is given to the bailiff there to distrain the same John so that he be at the next court to show how he holds the premises.

Amercement 16^{d} The homage there, namely: John Botery, Thomas Hunt, John Hiller, John Waker, William Legger and John Rydley in right of his wife, who, being sworn, present that William Wylde (8^{d}) in right of his wife, William May (2^{d}), Richard Knep (4^{d}) and Simon Glover (2^{d}) are suitors at court and make default. Therefore they remain in mercy as appears above their heads.

Death Also, they present that William Petley, who held freely of the lord a tenement and certain land, called Ballis, at a rent of $2^{s}3^{d}$, has died since the last court, and whether he has a brother or sister is not yet known; and who is his nearest heir is likewise not yet known. And therefore they have a day before

Day the next court to enquire better thereon.

Amercement 20^{d} Also, they present that Richard Gylis of Mitcham (20^{d}) overloads the common called le

c*um* ouib*us* suis i*de*o rem*anet* in M*iseri cord*ia p*r*out patet sup*er* eius Caput

affur*atum* p*er* homagi*um* tunc p*resens*

Ext*r*act*a* delib*erata* ballio

S*umm*a hui*us* Cur*ie* iij[s]

Heath with his sheep. Therefore he remains in mercy as appears above his head.

Affeered by the homage then present

Extract delivered to the bailiff

Amount of this court 3^s

Bandon	Cur*i*a Nich*ol*ai Carew Milit*is* tent*a* ib*id*em xv die Marcij anno regni Regis henrici Octaui vicesimo primo
Esson*i*um	Null*um*
Distr*ingere*	Cu*m* ad vltim*am* Cur*iam* dies dat*us* fuit Joh*anni* hyller vsq*ue* hanc Cur*iam* ad ostend*endam* euidenc*iam* quomodo tenet cert*am* terr*am* nup*er* Rob*er*ti Waker & non ven*it* *ideo* *pre*ceptu*m* est Ballio ib*idem* q*uo*d distr*ingat* eiusdem Joh*anne*m Jta q*uo*d sit ad p*roximam* Cur*iam* ad ostend*endum* quomodo p*re*missa tenet
M*isericord*ia xiiij[d]	Homagiu*m* ib*id*em videl*ice*t Joh*anne*s Botery Thomas hunt Joh*anne*s hyller Ric*ard*us knep Joh*anne*s Waker Wille*lmu*s legger & Joh*anne*s Redley qui Jur*ati* p*re*sent*ant* q*uo*d Wille*lmu*s Wylde (viij[d]) de Jure vx*or*is Wille*lmu*s May (ij[d]) Simon Glouer (ij[d]) & tenens terr*e* nup*er* Wille*lm*i petley (ij[d]) sunt sect*atores* Cur*ie* & fac*iunt* def*altam* *ideo* in M*isericord*ia rem*anent* p*ro*ut patet sup*er* eo*rum* Capit*a*
obit*us*	Jtem p*re*sent*ant* q*uo*d Joh*anne*s Sharnford qui de d*omi*no tenuit iure Margarete vx*or*is sue vnu*m* Mesuagiu*m* & clausu*m* terr*e* adiacen*s* contra vna*m* acr*am* p*er* reddit*um* ij[s] p*er* annu*m* obijt ip*s*aq*ue* Margareta ip*su*m sup*er*uixit que quid*em* Margaret*a* nunc nupt*a* est Thome Guster qui p*re*sens in Cur*i*a cogn*ovit* se tener*e* p*re*missa vt in Jure p*re*dic*t*e Margarete Et fec*it*
ffidelit*as*	ffidelit*atem*

andon A court of Nicholas Carew, knight, held there on the 15th day of March in the twenty-first year of the reign of King Henry VIII. 1530

ssoin None

istrain Whereas at the last court a day was given to John Hyller before this court to show evidence of how he holds certain land late of Robert Waker, and he did not come, therefore the order is given to the bailiff there to distrain the same John so that he be at the next court to show how he holds the premises.

mercement 14^{d} The homage there, namely: John Botery, Thomas Hunt, John Hyller, Richard Knep, John Waker, William Legger and John Redley, who, being sworn, present that William Wylde (8^{d}) in right of his wife, William May (2^{d}), Simon Glover (2^{d}) and the tenant of land late of William Petley (2^{d}) are suitors at court and make default. Therefore they remain in mercy as appears above their heads.

eath Also, they present that John Sharnford, who held of the lord in right of Margaret his wife a messuage and close of land lying against an acre at a rent of 2^{s} a year, has died and the same Margaret has survived him and the same Margaret is now married to Thomas Guster who, present in court, has acknowledged that he holds the premises as in right of the

ealty aforementioned Margaret. And he has done fealty.

ordinacio

Et ordinat*um* est t*am* p*er* autoritate*m* hui*us* Cur*ie* q*uam* p*er* assent*ationem* omni*um* tenen*cium* q*uo*d null*us* tenen*s* ponat aliqua ani*mal*ja in Co*mmun*ia ib*idem* nisi dat noticiam & concordat cu*m* pastore greg*um* ib*idem* Et si incorrar*ium* fecer*int* bene licebit p*re*fat*o* pastori ani*mal*ja p*re*dict*a* ad punifeld*am* ib*idem* ducere Et quili*be*t eo*rum* sub pena p*ro* quoli*be*t an*imalio* ij[d] Et sim*i*lit*er* ordinat*um* est q*uo*d null*us* tenens ducat nec reducat aliquos equos aut boues ad co*mmun*es campos in estate nisi ducat equos p*re*dic*t*os & boues p*re*dic*t*os iugat*os* quili*be*t eo*rum* sub pena p*ro* quoli*be*t equo & ani*malio* ij[d] Et [ ][1] non licebit alicui ponere aliquos porcos in co*mmun*ibus campis ante festu*m* Assumpcionis be*at*e Marie sub pen*a* p*ro* quoli*be*t porco ij[d]

S*umma* hui*us* Cur*ie* [ ]

[1] Illegible.

Order   And it is ordered, both by the authority of this court and by the assent of all the tenants, that no tenant shall put any animals on the common there unless he gives notice and agrees with the shepherd of the flocks there. And if they make a nuisance the aforementioned shepherd shall have full authority to take the aforementioned animals to the pound there, and each and every one of them under a penalty of 2^d for each and every beast. And likewise it is ordered that no tenant shall take any horses or oxen in or out of the common fields in summer unless he take the aforementioned horses and oxen yoked, each and every one of them under a penalty for each and every horse and animal of 2^d. And [ ] [1] no one shall be allowed to put any pigs in the common fields before the feast of the Assumption of the blessed Mary (15th August), under a penalty of 2^d for each and every pig.   1530

Amount of this court [ ]

Bandon	Cur*ia* Nich*ol*ai Carew Milit*is* tent*a* ib*i*d*e*m xxvij^{mo} die Januarij anno regni Regis henrici Octaui vicesimo s*e*c*un*do
Esson*ium*	Null*um*
M*iserico*r*d*ia xviij^{d}	Homagi*um* ib*i*d*e*m videl*ic*et Thomas hunt Joh*ann*es hyller sen*ior* Johannes Waker Will*elmus* legger & Joh*ann*es Rydley qui Jur*ati* p*r*esent*ant* q*uo*d Will*elmus* Wyllde (viij^{d}) Jur*e* vx*or*is Will*elmus* May (iiij^{d}) tenen*s* terr*e* nup*er* Will*elm*i Petley (ij^{d}) Ri*car*dus knepe (ij^{d}) Thomas Guster (ij^{d}) sunt sect*atores* Cur*ie* & ffac*iunt* def*altam* i*de*o in M*isericor*d*ia* rem*anent* p*r*out patet sup*er* eo*rum* Capit*a*

Bandon — A court of Nicholas Carew, knight, held there on the 27th day of January in the twenty-second year of the reign of King Henry VIII. 1531

Essoin — None

Amercement 18d — The homage there, namely: Thomas Hunt, John Hyller senior, John Waker, William Legger and John Rydley, who, being sworn, present that William Wyllde (8d) in right of his wife, William May (4d), the tenant of land late of William Petley (2d), Richard Knepe (2d), Thomas Guster (2d) are suitors at court and make default. Therefore they remain in mercy as appears above their heads.

Bandon Curi*a* pr*e*potentissimi & exellentissi*mi* do*mi*ni henr*ici* octaui dei gra*cia* Anglie Ffranc*ie* & hib*er*nie Regis ffidei defens*oris* & in terr*a* eccl*es*ie Anglic*ane* & hib*er*nice Sup*r*emi Capit*is* ib*idem* tent*a* ij[do] die Marcij anno regni sui xxvj[to]

Esson*ium* Null*um*

M*isericord*ia xvj[d] Homag*ium* ib*i*dem v*idelicet* Clemens hyller Joh*annes* Rydley Will*elmus* legger Joh*annes* Waker & Joh*annes* Will*i*ams qui Jur*ati* p*resentant* q*uo*d Will*elmus* Wylde (iiij[d]) Will*elmus* may de london (iiij[d]) humffrid*us* Collyns (iiij[d]) Thomas petley (iiij[d]) & Thom*as* Tompson (ij[d]) sunt Sect*atores* Cur*ie* & ffaciunt def*altam* i*de*o rem*anent* in m*isericord*ia quil*i*bet eo*rum* p*r*o*ut* p*atet* sup*er* eorum Capita

Cum discordia h*ab*ita & mot*a* est int*er* ffirmari*os* do*mi*ni Reg*is* & Rectorem de Bedyngton p*ro* vna pecia terr*e* jac*enti* in le Southffeld de Bedyngton ex p*ar*te occident*a*li vie Regie ib*i*dem ducent*is* a Bedyngton vers*us* wodcott continen*ti* circit*er* xiiij acr*as* terr*e* & homagiu*m* inde on*eretur* ad veritatem inde dicend*am* vt*er*um predict*a* pecia terr*e* p*er*tinet rectorie p*r*edict*e* an ne Qui Jur*ati* dicunt sup*er* sacr*amentum* suu*m* q*uo*d Rector de Bedyngton quond*a*m h*ab*uit vnu*m* Campum voc*atum* porcionaryffeld continent*em* circit*er* octo acr*as* mo*do* inclus*um* inffra p*ar*cu*m* de Bedyngton & tres acr*as* terr*e* eid*e*m Campo adiacent*is* similit*er* inclus*e* inffra p*redi*c*tum* parcum mo*do* voc*ate* New orchard Jn eius

Bandon A court of the most puissant and excellent Lord Henry VIII, by the grace of God King of England, France and Ireland, Defender of the Faith and, on earth, Supreme Head of the English and Irish Church, held there on the second day of March in the thirty-sixth year of his reign. 1545

Essoin None

Amercement 16^d The homage there, namely: Clement Hyller, John Rydley, William Legger, John Waker and John Williams, who, being sworn, present that William Wylde (4^d), William May of London (4^d), Humphrey Collyns (4^d), Thomas Petley (4^d) and Thomas Tompson (2^d) are suitors at court and make default. Therefore they remain in mercy, each of them as appears above his head.

Whereas a dispute has arisen and continues between the farmers of the Lord King and the rector of Beddington for a piece of land lying in the South Field of Beddington on the west side of the King's highway, there leading from Beddington towards Woodcote, containing about fourteen acres of land, and the homage is then charged to declare the truth thereon,whether the aforesaid piece of land belongs to the rectory aforesaid or not. They, being sworn, say upon their oath that the rector of Beddington formerly had a field called the Portionary Field containing about eight acres, now enclosed within the park of Beddington, and three acres of land lying next to the same

recompensaci*onem* & in escambium p*ro* p*redi*c*to* Campo & tribus [1] acr*is* p*re*dict*is* p*re*di*c*tus Rector h*ab*uit de Ric*ard*o Carew Milit*e* adtunc d*omi*no Man*e*rij p*re*dict*i* p*re*dict*am* peci*am* terr*e* iacent*em* in Southffeld p*redi*c*t*a iux*ta* viam p*redi*c*t*am

Cog*nitio* tenure

Jt*em* p*re*sent*ant* q*uo*d Joh*ann*es Rydley & Joh*ann*a vx*or* eius nup*er* vx*or* Joh*ann*is Dabou*r*ne qui coniuncti*m* tenuer*unt* in iure ip*s*ius Joh*ann*e vnu*m* Ten*emen*t*u*m cum Gardino adiacent*i* nup*er* Elene Skete iac*ens* in Bedyngton p*er* redd*i*t*um* xx[d] p*er* annu*m* qui qu*i*d*e*m Joh*ann*es obijt ip*s*aq*ue* Joh*ann*a ip*s*um sup*er*uixit que p*re*sens in Cur*ia* cogn*ovit* tenere p*re*missa de d*omi*no p*er* redd*i*t*um* p*redi*c*t*um & alia s*e*ruic*ia* & ffecit d*omi*no ffidelit*atem*

reddit*um* ffidelit*as*

S*u*mm*a* huiu*s* Cur*ie* xvj[d]

1 MS: tres.

field, likewise enclosed within the aforesaid park, now called the New Orchard. In recompense of, and exchange for, the aforesaid field and three [1] acres aforesaid, the aforesaid rector had of Richard Carew, knight, at that time lord of the manor aforesaid, the aforesaid piece of land lying in the South Field aforesaid next to the aforesaid highway. 1545

cknowledgement of tenure

Also, they present that John Rydley and Joan his wife, late wife of John Dabourne, who held jointly, in right of the same Joan, a tenement with a garden adjacent, late of Helen Skete, lying in Beddington, for a rent of 20^{d} a year, and the same John has died, whom the same Joan survived, and she, present in court, has acknowledged that she holds the premises of the lord for the rent aforesaid and other services. And she did fealty to the lord.

Rent
Fealty

Amount of this court 16^{d}

Bedyngton

Cur*ia* *pre*potentissimi & exellentissi*mi* d*om*ini henrici octaui dei gra*cia* anglie ffranc*ie* & hib*er*nie Regis ffidei defens*oris* & in terr*a* eccl*es*ie anglic*ane* & hib*er*nice Supremi Capit*is* ib*id*em tent*a* ij[do] die Marcij Anno regni eiusd*em* d*omi*ni Regis xxxvj[to]

Esson*ium*

Null*um*

m*isericord*ia xij[d]

Homagiu*m* ib*id*em videl*ice*t d*omi*nus Will*elmu*s Howerd (non monit*us*) Garthus ffromans (ij[d]) kat*er*ina Skynner (non monit*a*) Will*elmu*s Dausten (ij[d]) Rector de Bedyngton (ij[d]) petrus Bonedyke (ij[d]) Joh*anne*s A Gate (ij[d]) henr*icus* Staplerst [1] (non monit*us*) tenens terr*e* nup*er* Thome Carter (ij[d]) solemnit*er* exact*i* non comp*ar*uer*unt* ad hunc die*m* i*de*o ipsi rem*anent* in m*isericord*ia prout p*atet* super eor*um* Capit*a*

distr*ingere* [v*e*l inp*re*ceder*e*] [2]

Adhuc p*re*ceptum est distr*ingere* tenent*es* terre nup*er* henrici hewett in cert*a* terr*a* voc*ata* lakelond tam p*ro* Releuio d*omi*no acciden*ti* p*er* mort*em* Thome hewett q*ua*m pro Reluio & h*er*iett*o* d*omi*no acciden*tibus* p*er* mort*em* d*ic*t*i* henr*ici* & preceptu*m* est Ballio distr*ingere* Garth*um* ffromans in cert*is* terr*is* suis p*ro* Releuio domino acciden*ti* p*er* mort*em* p*at*ris sui

S*umma* hui*us* Curi*e* xij[d]

1 ij[d] cancelled.

2 This reading is not beyond question and no satisfactory translation of it has been found.

Beddington A court of the most puissant and excellent Lord Henry VIII, by the grace of God King of England, France and Ireland, Defender of the Faith and, on earth, Supreme Head of the English and Irish Church, held there on the 2nd day of March in the thirty-sixth year of the same king's reign. 1545

Essoin None

Amercement 12d The homage there, namely: Lord William Howerd (not informed); Garth Fromans (2d); Katherine Skynner (not informed); William Dausten (2d); the rector of Beddington (2d); Peter Bonedyke (2d); John Agate (2d); Henry Staplerst [1] (not informed); the tenant of the land formerly Thomas Carter's (2d), solemnly summoned, did not appear on this day. Therefore they remain in mercy as appears above their heads.

Distrain [for] At this time the order is given to distrain the tenants of land formerly Henry Hewett's [ ][2] on a certain area called Lakeland, both for the relief falling to the lord through the death of Thomas Hewett and for the relief and heriot falling to the lord through the death of the said Henry. And the order is given to the bailiff to distrain Garth Fromans on certain of his lands for the relief falling to the lord through the death of his father.

Amount of this court 12d

Bedyngton

Vis*us* ffranc*i*pleg*ii* cum Curi*a* p*re*potentiss*imi* & exellentissi*mi* d*omi*ni henr*ici* octaui dei gra*cia* anglie ffranc*ie* & hibe*r*nie Re*gis* ffidei defens*oris* & in terr*a* eccl*es*ie anglic*ane* & hibe*r*nic*e* Sup*r*emi Capit*is* ib*idem* tent*a* xv die Junij anno regni eiusd*em* d*omi*ni Re*gis* tricesimo Septimo

Horley

Joh*ann*es Agate decenar*ius* ib*idem* & ceter*i* inh*abi*t*antes* solempnit*er* exact*i* non comp*ar*uer*unt* ad hunc vis*um* sed ffecer*unt* def*altam* *tame*n non adm*er*ciant*ur* qu*o*d non moniti ffuerunt

Rysyndon

*C*ommun*is* ffinis xij^{d}

Will*elmu*s Brokhole decenar*ius* ib*ide*m solempnit*er* exact*us* non comp*ar*uit m*odo* dicunt q*uo*d infirm*us* est & misit p*er* Joh*ann*em pynner Const*abularium* ib*ide*m xii^{d} de cert*a* C*ommun*i fin*e* ib*ide*m ad hunc die*m* & cet*er*i inh*abi*t*antes* ib*ide*m non monit*i* ffuer*unt* id*eo* non adm*er*ciant*ur*

Bedyngton

*C*ommun*is* ffinis iij^{s}

Joh*anne*s Waker (ij^{d}) vn*ũs* [1] decenar*ius* ib*ide*m solempnit*er* exact*us* non comp*ar*uit *ide*o rem*anet* in m*isericord*ia & Garthus Dewbere alter decenar*ius* ib*ide*m ven*it* & for*is* p*resentauit* de cert*a* C*ommun*i ffin*e* ad hunc die*m* iij^{s} & Q*uo*d Will*elmu*s Dewman est residens ib*ide*m & ffacit def*altam* vis*us* & q*uo*d vxor Joh*ann*is horwald (vj^{d}) est C*ommun*is pistor panis & vend*it* pan*em* minor*em* ass*is*e d*omi*ni R*egis* & q*uo*d henr*icus* Gaynysford (xvj^{d}) vend*it*

[1] MS: vni*us*

Beddington — A view of frankpledge with the court of the most puissant and excellent Lord Henry VIII, by the grace of God King of England, France and Ireland, Defender of the Faith and, on earth, Supreme Head of the English and Irish Church, held there on the 15th day of June in the thirty-seventh year of the same Lord King's reign. 1545

Horley — John Agate, tything-man there, and the other inhabitants, solemnly summoned, did not appear at this view but made default. However, they are not in mercy because they were not informed.

Rysyndon — William Brokhole, tything-man there, solemnly summoned, did not appear, they now say because he was ill, and on this day he sent 12^{d} there
Common fine 12^{d} — by John Pynner, constable there, for a certain common fine. And the other inhabitants there were not informed and therefore are not in mercy.

Beddington — John Waker (2^{d}), one [1] tything-man there, solemnly summoned, did not appear. Therefore he remains in mercy. And Garth Dewbere, the
Common fine 3^{s} — other tything-man there, came and presented 3^{s} in public for a certain common fine and *presented*: that William Dewman is resident there and makes default of view; and that the wife of John Horwald (6^{d}) is a public bread baker and sells a loaf smaller than *that of* the Lord King's assize; and that Henry

pan*em* factu*m* de peut*er*wrue [1] & insalubr*em*
& q*uo*d idem henr*icus* (ij^{s}) vend*it* Bera*m*
insalubre*m* & q*uo*d vescell*a* ip*s*ius henr*ici*
non custod*unt* mensura*m* iux*ta* fforma*m* Statuti
& Joh*anne*s Bank*es* ffecit insult*am* Ni*cholao*
Glover & ip*s*um verberauit & maletotauit cont*ra*
pace*m* d*omi*ni Re*gis* *ide*o ip*s*i rem*anent* in

*Misericord*ia v^{s}x^{d} — m*isericord*ia quil*ib*et eo*rum* p*ro*ut p*atet* sup*er*
eius Capud

xij Jur*ati* ib*idem* — Videl*ice*t Will*elmu*s legger Const*abularius*
Clemens hyller Nich*ola*us Broke Simon Shott
Joh*anne*s Chamberlen Joh*anne*s Woneham Ric*ard*us
Glover Thom*a*s Brampton Ric*ard*us kechyn
Joh*anne*s Bank*es* Thom*a*s Roger Nich*olau*s Newbery
andr*ew* young & Joh*anne*s Rakleid qui Jurati [2]
dicunt sup*er* sacr*amentu*m suu*m* q*uo*d decenar*ii*
p*re*no*m*inati bene & ffidelit*er* p*re*sent*ave*r*unt*
& null*um* ffecerunt Concell*um* & vlt*er*ius
p*resentant* quod h*abi*tantes de Bedyngton
p*er*mittunt via*m* Regis vocat*am* pyttlent ffore

Dies pene — ffunderat*am* qui h*ab*ent die*m* exavuend*am* via*m*
illa*m* cit*ra* p*ro*x*imu*m vis*um* sub p*ena* vj^{s}viij^{d}
& q*uo*d vnus equus color gray p*re*cij xx^{d} vlt*ra*

[ ] [3] ffor*is* xx^{d} — Custod*iam* in Custodiam [ ] [4] hervy
prouenien*s* in d*omi*nium de ext*remo* ad ffest*um*
Pentecost*is* per annu*m* & die*m* elaps*os* & q*uia*
null*us* inffra annum & die*m* oposuit aut
clamau*it* i*de*o adiudicato d*omi*no tanq*ua*m fforis

1 This word has not been satisfactorily identified.
2 p*re*sent*ant* cancelled.
3 Illegible.
4 Illegible.

Gaynysford (16^{d}) sells unwholesome bread 1545
made of [ ][1]; and that the same Henry (2^{s}) sells unwholesome beer; and that this Henry's containers do not keep the measure according to the form of the statute; and *that* John Bankes assaulted Nicholas Glover and beat him and ill-treated him against the
Amercement $5^{s}10^{d}$ Lord King's peace. Therefore they remain in mercy, each of them for the amount appearing above his head.

Twelve sworn there — Namely: William Legger, constable; Clement Hyller; Nicholas Broke; Simon Shott; John Chamberlen; John Woneham; Richard Glover; Thomas Brampton; Richard Kechyn; John Bankes; Thomas Roger; Nicholas Newbery; Andrew Young and John Rakleid. These, sworn,[2] say on their oath that the tything-men aforementioned presented well and faithfully and made no concealment. And furthermore, they present that the inhabitants of Beddington agree to put through the King's highway, called Pyttlent,
Penalty day — which is to be laid, and a day has been appointed before the next view for the digging of that road, under penalty of $6^{s}8^{d}$. And that
[ ][3] stray 20^{d} — a grey horse, value 20^{d}, straying out of custody into the custody of [ ][4] Hervy, from outside into the demesne, at the feast of Pentecost (1st June, 1544), a year and a day having passed, and because no one within that

elecio *officiis*

& in officio Joh*ann*is Waker vni*us* decenar*ii* ib*ide*m elegeru*nt* Thoma*m* Brampton & in officio Const*abularii* ib*ide*m elegeru*nt* Simon*em* Shott qui jur*ati* sunt in eisde*m* officijs

S*umma* hui*us* vis*us* & Cur*ie* xj^{s}vj^d
S*umma* tot*a* Cur*ie* xvij^{s}vj^d
Vi*delicet* de Commun*i* ffini iiij^s
[ ][1] xx^d
amerc*iamento* xjx^{s}x^d

[1] Illegible.

year and a day opposed *this* or claimed *it* it 1545
has therefore been awarded to the lord as a stray.

lection to ffices

And to the office of John Waker, a tything-man, there, they elected Thomas Brampton. And to the office of constable there they elected Simon Shott. They were sworn in the same offices.

Amount of this view and court		$11^{s}6^{d}$
Full amount of the court		$17^{s}6^{6}$
Namely:	Common fine	4^{s}
	[ ] [1]	20^{d}
	Amercement	$19^{s}10^{d}$

Bandon	Cur*ia* pre*p*otentiss*i*mi & exellentiss*i*mi d*omi*ni henr*ici* viij dei gra*cia* anglie ffranc*ie* & hibe*r*nie Regis fidei defens*oris* & in terr*a* eccl*es*ie anglic*ane* & hibe*r*nice su*p*rem*i* Ca*p*it*is* ib*ide*m tent*a* sexto die a*p*rilis anno Regni sui tricesimo se*p*timo
Esson*ium*	Null*um*
M*isericord*ia xxij^{d}	homag*ium* ib*ide*m videl*ice*t Clemenci*us* hyller Joh*ann*es Waker & Joh*ann*es Will*i*ams qui Jur*ati* *pr*esent*ant* q*uo*d tenen*s* terr*e* nu*per* Wille*lm*i Wylde (iiij^{d}) Wille*lm*us May de london (iiij^{d}) humfrid*us* Collett (iiij^{d}) Thomas *p*etley (iiij^{d}) Thomas Tompson (iiij^{d}) & Joh*ann*a Rydley vid*ua* (ij^{d}) sunt sect*atores* Cur*ie* & ffaciunt def*altam* id*e*o rem*anent* in m*isericord*ia quil*i*bet eor*um* *pro*ut p*atet* sup*er* eius Ca*p*ut
Obitus Wille*lm*i legger	Jtem *pr*esent*ant* q*uo*d Wille*lm*us legger qui de d*omi*no tenuit libe*r*e vnu*m* Ten*eme*ntu*m* & xxvj acr*as* terr*e* nu*per* wille*lm*i legger *p*at*ris* sui iac*entes* in Bedyngton *per* redd*itum* ij^{s}iij^{d} *per* annu*m* obijt *p*ost vltim*am* Cur*iam* inde sei*situs*
he*r*iettu*m* vj^{s}viij^{d} Releuiu*m* ij^{s}iij^{d} Distr*ingere* *pro* ffidelit*ate*	*p*ost cuiu*s* morte*m* accid*it* d*omi*no de he*r*iett*o* vnus equus Cast*ratus* *pre*cij vj^{s}viij^{d} Et q*uo*d Joh*ann*es legger est eius fili*us* & heres & vadiauit d*omi*no ij^{s}iij^{d} de Releuio suo d*omi*no debit*o* *per* morte*m* d*icti* Wille*lm*i legger *p*at*ris* sui Et *pre*ceptu*m* est distr*ingere* eundem Joh*anne*m *pro* ffidelit*ate* cit*ra* *pro*xi*mam* Cur*iam*
Alienacio	Jtem *pr*esent*ant* q*uo*d Wille*lm*us Wylde qui de d*omi*no tenuit libe*r*e in Jure Dorothie vx*or*is

andon

A court of the most puissant and excellent Lord Henry VIII, by the grace of God King of England, France and Ireland, Defender of the Faith and, on earth, Supreme Head of the English and Irish Church, held there on the 6th day of April in the thirty-seventh year of his reign. 1546

ssoin

None

mercement 22^{d}

The homage there, namely: Clement Hyller, John Waker and John Williams, who, being sworn, present that the tenant of land late of William Wylde (4^{d}), William May of London (4^{d}), Humphrey Collett (4^{d}), Thomas Petley (4^{d}), Thomas Tompson (4^{d}) and Joan Rydley, widow (2^{d}), are suitors at court and make default. Therefore they remain in mercy, each of them as appears above his head.

eath of illiam egger

Also, they present that William Legger, who held freely of the lord a tenement and twenty-six acres of land, late of William Legger his father, lying in Beddington, for a rent of $2^{s}3^{d}$ a year, has died seised thereof since the last court, after whose death there fell to the lord

eriot $6^{s}8^{d}$

as heriot a gelding worth $6^{s}8^{d}$; and that John

elief $2^{s}3^{d}$

Legger is his son and heir and has paid to the lord $2^{s}3^{d}$ as his relief, due to the lord

istrain or ealty

through the death of the said William Legger his father. And the order is given to distrain the same John for fealty before the next court.

lienation

Also, they present that William Wylde, who held freely of the lord, in right of Dorothy his wife, sue vnum tenementum cum iij acris terre in Bandonfeld ij acras & dimidiam & aliam dimidiam Acram iacentes in Wallyngtonfeld per redditum xij^{d} per annum & vnam aliam acram terre iacentem Wallyngtonfeld per redditum iiij^{d} per annum vnum aliud tenementum nuper Willelmi lythyer iacens iuxta molendinum per redditum iiij^{s} per annum vnum aliud tenementum cum certa terra eidem iacenti in Bedyngton predicto quondam Thome Wardham vocatum lokyers per redditum ij^{s}iiij^{d} per annum ac certam terram vocatam Dogges nuper dicti Thome Wardham per redditum xiij^{s}iiij^{d} per annum tamen iamdudum soluit nisi x^{s} premissa vendidit & alienauit Rogero Copley militi & heredibus

Distringere — suis quem preceptum est distringere tam pro fidelitate quam pro redditu predicto relevio citra proximam Curiam

Ordinacio sub pena — Ad hanc Curiam Ordinatum est tam auctoritate huius Curie quam per assensum omnium tenencium adtunc presencium quod nullus infra dominium decetero custodiat aliquos porcos transeuntes extra suum separcelle nisi Sint annulati & Justificati sub pena pro quolibet porco vj^{d} Et quod bene licebit Ballio ibidem quod distringat & imparcare faciat omnes illos porcos sic inuentos insigillatos & ibidem eos detinere quousque pena pro [1] illis sic fforis soluta sit

Summa huius curie x^{s}ix^{d} tum vj^{s}viij^{d} de herietto
[ ] [2] & xxij^{d} de amerciamento

1 MS: per

2 Illegible.

a tenement with three acres of land in Bandon Field, two and a half acres and another half acre lying in Wallington Field, for a rent of 12^{d} a year; and another acre of land lying *in* Wallington Field for a rent of 4^{d} a year; another tenement, late of William Lythyer, lying next to the mill for a rent of 4^{s} a year; another tenement with certain land adjacent in Beddington aforesaid, formerly of Thomas Wardham, called Lockyers, for a rent of $2^{s}4^{d}$ a year, and certain land called Dogges, late of the said Thomas Wardham, for a rent of $13^{s}4^{d}$ a year. Although he paid long since, save for 10^{s}, he sold and alienated the premises to Roger Copley, knight, and his heirs. The order is given to distrain him, both for the fealty and the rent *and* for the aforementioned relief before the next court. 1546

istrain

rder under enalty

At this court it is ordered, both by the authority of this court and with the assent of all the tenants then present, that no one within the lordship shall henceforth keep any pigs wandering outside his holding unless they are ringed and licensed, under a penalty for each and every pig of 6^{d}; and that the bailiff there has full authority to distrain and have impounded all those pigs found thus, unmarked, and to detain them there until the fine for [1] their straying thus is paid.

Amount of this court $10^{s}9^{d}$ then $6^{s}8^{d}$ for heriot
[ ] [2] & 22^{d} for amercement

Bedyngton

Visus ffranc*i*pleg*ii* pr*e*potentissimi & exellentissimi d*omi*ni henrici octaui dei gra*cia* anglie ffranc*ie* & hib*er*nie Regis ffidei defens*oris* & in terr*a* eccl*es*ie anglic*ane* & hib*er*nice Sup*re*mi Capit*is* ib*ide*m tent*a* xviij die Junij anno regni d*i*ct*i* d*omi*ni Regis tricesimo octauo

horley

Joh*ann*es A Gate decenar*ius* ibidem & ceteri inh*abitantes* ib*ide*m (xij^{d}) solempnit*er* exac*t*i non comp*ar*uer*unt* ad hunc die*m* sed fecer*unt* defalt*am* *ide*o rem*anent* in m*isericord*ia p*ro*ut p*atet* sup*er* eor*um* Capit*a*

Chesruden
Commun*is*
fin*is* xij^{d}
M*isericord*ia
xij^{d}

Will*elmus* Brokhole decenar*ius* ibidem ven*it* cum decen*aria* sua & Jur*atus* p*re*sent*auit* de cert*a* co*mmuni* fin*i* ad hunc die*m* iij^{s} Et qu*o*d henric*us* [ ][1] (ij^{d}) letus asshe (ij^{d}) Nich*ol*aus Wryvyn (ij^{d}) Will*elmus* yong (ij^{d}) & Joh*ann*es Mathew (ij^{d}) sunt residen*tes* ib*ide*m & faciunt def*altam* Et qu*o*d N[ ][2] lane (ij^{d}) est co*mmun*is br*ueri*us s*er*uic*ia* & ffregit assis*a*m d*omi*ni Reg*is* *ide*o rem*ane*t in m*isericord*ia p*ro*ut p*atet* sup*er* eius Caput

Bedyngton
Co*mmun*is
fin*is* iij^{s}

M*isericord*ia
xij^{d}

Thom*as* Brampton Decenar*ius* ib*ide*m ven*it* cum decen*aria* sua & Jur*atus* p*resentavit* de cert*a* co*mmuni* fin*i* p*er* Capit*a* ad hunc die*m* iij^{s} Et qu*o*d [ ][3] & Georg*ius* Apostell (ij^{d}) sunt residen*tes* ib*ide*m & faciunt def*altam* Et qu*o*d [ ] hurlok (vj^{d}) est

1 Illegible.
2 Illegible.
3 Illegible.

ɜeddington

A view of frankpledge of the most puissant and excellent Lord Henry VIII, by the grace of God King of England, France and Ireland, Defender of the Faith and, on earth, Supreme Head of the English and Irish Church, held there on the 18th day of June in the thirty-eighth year of the said Lord King's reign. 1546

ɪorley

John Agate, tything-man there, and the other inhabitants there (12^d), solemnly summoned, did not appear on this day but made default. Therefore they remain in mercy for the amount appearing above their heads.

'hesruden
'ommon
'ine 12^d
.mercement
12^d

William Brokhole, tything-man there, came with his frankpledge group and, sworn, presented 3^s on this day for a certain common fine and *presented*: that Henry [ ] [1] (2^d), Letus Asshe (2^d), Nicholas Wryvyn (2^d), William Yong (2^d) and John Mathew (2^d) are resident there and make default; and that N[ ] [2] Lane (2^d) is a public brewer by trade and breaks the Lord King's assize. Therefore he remains in mercy for the amount appearing above his name.

eddington
ommon
ine 3^s

nercement
12^d

Thomas Brampton, tything-man there, came with his frankpledge group and, sworn, presented 3^s on this day for a certain common per capita fine and *presented*: that [ ] [3] and George Apostell (2^d) are resident there and make default; and that

com*mun*is pistor panis & vend*it* pan*em* [minorem] assis*e* d*omi*ni R*egis* Et quod Rob*er*tus Yard*es* (ij[d]) est tipill*ator* s*er*uic*ia* & fregit assis*a*m d*omi*ni Regis *id*eo rem*anent* in m*isericord*ia p*r*out p*atet* sup*er* eoru*m* [Capita]

Residuu*m* huius vis*us* p*atet* in Dorso isti*us* Rot*u*li

xij Jur*ati* ib*id*em

V*idelice*t Simon Shott Const*abularius* Clemenci*us* hyller Joh*ann*es Waker Nich*ol*aus Broke Rob*er*tus Brampton Andr*ew* Yong Nich*ol*aus [ ] [1] Ric*ard*us kychyn Joh*ann*es Glover Thomas Roger Robertus hewett Thomas Gudchylde & Wille*lmus* Wodman qui pr*esentes* dicunt sup*er* sacram*entum* suu*m* q*uo*d decenar*ii* predicti bene & fidelit*er* present*averunt* & nullum fecer*unt* Concell*um* Et vlterius p*r*esent*ant* q*uo*d omnes tenent*es* de

Dies pene

Chysynden h*ab*ent*es* aliquas terr*as* int*er* p*ar*sons acre & pynners Close h*ab*ent die*m* escur*ere* foss*as* suas ib*id*em cit*ra* ff*es*t*u*m s*anc*ti Michael*is* arch*angel*i sub pe*na* quilibet eor*um* p*ro* quol*ibe*t p*ar*ticu*lare* iiij[d] Et q*uo*d inh*abi*t*antes* de Bedyngton permittunt scopas suas fore irreparatas qui h*ab*ent die*m* faciend*as* scopas ill*as* cit*ra* p*roximum* vis*um* sub pe*na* iij[s]iiij[d] Et q*uo*d Nich*ol*aus Broke pe*r*mittit Ramos arbor*is* sui sup*er*crescere via*m* Regia*m* erga terr*am* voc*atam* Surreys qui h*ab*et die*m* amputand*os* ramos p*r*ed*i*ct*os* citra f*es*t*u*m s*an*cte Margaret*e* sub p*ena* xx[d]

[1] Illegible.

/‾ _/ Hurlok (6^d) is a public bread baker and sells bread which is smaller than *that of* the Lord King's assize; and that Robert Yardes (2^d) is a wine and ale retailer by trade and breaks the Lord King's assize. Therefore they remain in mercy for the amount appearing above their heads. 1546

The rest of this view appears on the back of this roll.

Twelve men sworn there

Namely: Simon Shott, constable; Clemence Hyller; John Waker; Nicholas Broke; Robert Brampton; Andrew Yong; Nicholas /‾ _/ [1] Richard Kychyn; John Glover; Thomas Roger; Robert Hewett; Thomas Gudchylde and William Wodman. These, present, say on their oath that the aforementioned tything-men presented well and faithfully and made no concealment. And furthermore they present that all the

Penalty day

tenants of Chessington who have any land between Parson's Acre and Pynner's Close have been set a day before the feast of Saint Michael the Archangel (29th September) to clean out their ditches there, under penalty for each of them for each particular *offence* of 4^d; and that the inhabitants of Beddington who allow their shovels to remain unrepaired have been set a day before the next view to repair those shovels, under penalty of 3^s4^d; and that Nicholas Broke, who allows the branches of his tree to grow over the King's highway in the direction of the land called Surreys, has been set a day to cut off the

& in officio Const*abularii* de Chysynden
eleger*unt* Will*elm*um Brokhole
Et in officio decen*arii* ibidem elegerunt
Thoma*m* Gudchylde

Jur*ati* sunt in eisdem offic*iis*

	Clemenc*ius* hyller	
affuer*unt*	Nich*ol*aus Broke	Jur*ati*
	Rob*er*tus hewett	

Su*mma* hui*us* vis*us* vij^s^
tu*m* iiij^s^ de co*mmuni* fin*e* &
iij^s^ de am*erciamento*

aforementioned branches before the feast of Saint Margaret (20th July) under penalty of 20d. 1546

And they elected William Brokhole to the office of constable of Chessington.
And they elected Thomas Gudchylde to the office of tything-man there.

Sworn in these offices

	Clement Hyller	
Affeered	Nicholas Broke	Sworn
	Robert Hewett	

Amount of this view 7s
then 4s for common fine and
3s for amercement

Bandon

Cur*ia* pr*e*potentissimi & excellentissimi d*omi*ni Edwardi Sexti dei gra*cia* anglie ffranc*ie* & hib*er*nie Regis fidei defensoris & in terra eccl*es*ie Anglicane & hib*er*nice Supr*e*mi Capit*is* ib*id*em tent*a* xxiij° die Aprilis Anno regni Sui tercio

Esson*ia*

Joh*ann*es Woneh*a*m p*er* Rob*er*t*u*m hyller
Thomas petley p*er* Joh*ann*em legger

M*isericord*ia
x[d]

Homagiu*m* ib*id*em videl*ice*t Joh*ann*es Waker Joh*ann*es legger & Rob*er*t*us* hyller qui Jur*ati* pr*e*sent*ant* qu*o*d Rogerus Copley Myles (iiij[d]) Wille*lmu*s Maye de london (ij[d]) tenen*s* terr*e* nup*er* Rob*er*ti hunte (ij[d]) & Thomas Thompson (ij[d]) sunt sect*atores* Cur*ie* ib*id*em & faciunt def*altam* sect*e* sue Cur*ie* *ide*o in m*isericordi*a pr*o*ut p*atet* sup*er* eo*rum* Capit*a* & *cetera*

Dies
pe*ne*

Jt*e*m pr*e*sent*ant* qu*o*d henricus kneppe sup*er*on*er*at Co*mmuni*am voc*atam* Bandon Comen cum anim*ali*js suis ad pr*e*iud*icium* Dom*i*ni & tenenc*ium* ib*id*em Qui h*a*bet diem qu*o*d non amplius sup*er*on*er*at co*mmuni*am ill*am* sub pena xx[s]

S*umma* hui*us* Cur*ie* x[d]

Bandon A court of the most puissant and excellent Lord Edward VI, by the grace of God King of England, France and Ireland, Defender of the Faith and, on earth, Supreme Head of the English and Irish Church, held there on the 23rd day of April in the third year of his reign. 1549

Essoins John Woneham by Robert Hyller
Thomas Petley by John Legger

Amercement 10^d The homage there, namely: John Waker, John Legger and Robert Hyller, who, being sworn, present that Roger Copley, knight (4^d), William Maye of London (2^d), the tenant of land late of Robert Hunte (2^d) and Thomas Thompson (2^d) are suitors at court there and make default of their suit at court. Therefore they are in mercy as appears above their heads.

Penalty day Also, they present that Henry Kneppe overloads the common called Bandon Common with his beasts to the prejudice of the lord and of the tenants there. He has a day by which he shall no longer overload that common, under penalty of 20^s.

Amount of this court 10^d

Bedyngton Cur*ia* ib*id*em tent*a* die & anno sup*ra*dict*is*

Null*us* ib*id*em Comp*ar*uit *quo*d non moniti fuer*unt* & *cetera*

Beddington A court held there on the day and in the year mentioned above (23rd April, 1549).

No one appeared there because they were not warned etc..

Bandon Prima Curia Domini Thome Darcye ordinis garterij militis Domini Camerarij Hospicij prepotentissimi & excellentissimi domini Edwardi Sexti Regis Anglie tenta ibidem viij^{uo} die Octobris Anno Regni dicti domini Regis sexto

Essonium

[1] Ad hanc Curiam venerunt Ricardus Wood Johannes Wooneham Johannes Waker Johannes Lake Johannes lyggerd [2] Robertus hiller & Thomas Pettley & fecerunt Domino fidelitatem pro terris suis quas tenent de manerio predicto

Homagium ibidem videlicet Ricardus Wod Johannes Woneham Johannes Waker Johannes Lake Johannes liggerd Robertus hiller & Thomas Pettley Qui Jurati presentant quod Domina Elizabeth Copley vidua (iiij^{d}) Willelmus Maye de london (iiij^{d}) tenens terre [3] Thome Hunt (ij^{d}) & Thomas Thompson (ij^{d}) sunt sectatores Curie & faciunt Defaltam secte sue Curie ideo remanent in misericordia prout & cetera

Alienacio Jtem presentant quod Margareta vxor Johannis Williams que de domino tenuit libere vnum tenementum cum paruo clauso adiacenti continenti circiter vnam acram terre iacentem

[1] Homagium ibidem videlicet cancelled.
[2] & cancelled.
[3] nuper cancelled.

Bandon The first court of Lord Thomas Darcye, knight of the Order of the Garter, Lord Chamberlain of the household of the most puissant and excellent Lord Edward VI, King of England, held there on the 8th day of October in the sixth year of the reign of the said Lord King. 1552

Essoin

[1] To this court came Richard Wood, John Wooneham, John Waker, John Lake, John Lyggerd, [2] Robert Hiller and Thomas Pettley and did fealty to the lord for their lands which they hold of the aforementioned manor.

The homage there, namely: Richard Wod, John Woneham, John Waker, John Lake, John Liggerd, Robert Hiller and Thomas Pettley, who, being sworn, present that the Lady Elizabeth Copley, widow (4^d), William Maye of London (4^d), the tenant of land [3] of Thomas Hunt (2^d) and Thomas Thompson (2^d) are suitors at court and make default of their suit at court. Therefore they remain in mercy etc..

Alienation Also, they present that Margaret, the wife of John Williams, who held freely of the lord a tenement with a small close adjacent containing about an acre of land lying in Bandon for a

in Bandon *per* redditu*m* ij[s] *per* Annu*m* obijt post vltim*am* Cur*iam* inde se*isita per* Cui*us* morte*m* n*ihil* accid*it* Dom*in*o de her*ietto* quia ni*hil* Coop*ertum* Et q*uo*d Thom*as* lewes est eius filius & heres & plene etatis Qui [1] quid*em* Thom*as* Lewes p*re*miss*a* alienauit cuid*am* Joh*anni* lewes & her*edibus* suis p*ro*ut p*er* cart*am* sua*m* in plen*a* Cur*ia* ostensa*m* pleni*us* liquet Qui quid*em* Joh*annes* p*re*sens in Cur*ia* cogn*ovit* tenere premiss*a* p*er* Reddit*um* p*re*d*ictum* & fec*it* fidelitat*em* Et vadiauit d*om*ino de Releuio ij[s]

fidel*itas* sol*utum* ballio in Cur*ia* Rel*e*vium ij[s]

pen*a* for*is*

Jt*e*m pr*esent*ant q*uo*d cum Nich*ol*aus Colgate (vj[s]viij[d]) h*ab*uit die*m* ad vltim*am* Cur*iam* q*uo*d ne ampli*us* [2] sup*er*one*r*et comm*un*em campu*m* voc*atum* Sowthfeld modo dicunt sup*er* sacr*amentum* suu*m* q*uo*d p*re*dic*t*us Nich*ol*aus ex illo temp*o*re sup*er*one*r*auit & adhuc sup*er*one*r*at campu*m* illu*m* anim*ali*js porcis & equis suis i*de*o incurr*it* pen*am* Et h*ab*et die*m* vlt*e*riore*m* q*uo*d ne ampli*us* [3] custod*iat* aliquos porcos vlt*ra* ff*estum* Nat*ivi*t*a*tis d*omi*ni p*roximum* sub pen*a* p*ro* quol*i*bet porco xl[d] Et q*uo*d non custod*iat* aliqua anim*alia* sup*er* le downe voc*atum* le Sheppasture sub pen*a* p*ro* quol*i*bet anim*al*io vj[s]viij[d]

Jt*e*m q*uo*d Nich*ol*aus Broke (xl[d]) & Joh*annes*

1 p*re*sens in cancelled.

2 eun cancelled.

3 ita fac*iat* sub pen*a* cancelled.

rent of 2^s a year, died after the last court seised thereof, by whose death nothing fell to the lord as heriot because nothing was found; and that Thomas Lewes is her son and heir and of full age. And the same Thomas Lewes [1] alienated the premises to a certain John Lewes and his heirs, as by his charter, shown in open court, he more fully makes clear. And the same John, present in court, acknowledged that he holds the premises for the aforementioned rent and did fealty. And he paid to the lord 2^s as relief. 1552

Fealty Paid to the bailiff in Court
2^s relief

Penalty for outdoor offences

Also, they present that since Nicholas Colgate (6^s8^d) had a day at the last court by which he should no longer [2] overload the common field called South Field, now they say on their oath that the aforementioned Nicholas from that time overloaded, and up to the present overloads, that field with his animals, pigs and horses, therefore he incurs the penalty. And he has a further day by which he shall no longer [3] keep any pigs after the feast of the Nativity of the Lord next, under penalty of 40^d for each and every pig. And that he shall not keep any animals on le Down, called le Sheep Pasture, under a penalty, for each and every animal, of 6^s8^d.

Also, that Nicholas Broke (40^d) and John Blake

Blake (xl^{d}) qui destrux*erunt* grana tenenc*ium* in *commun*ibus campis ib*idem* i*de*o rem*anent* in *misericord*ia p*r*o*u*t & *cetera*

Ad h*a*nc Cur*iam* ordinat*um* est t*a*m Aucthoritat*e* hui*us* Cur*ie* q*uam* assensu om*nium* tenenc*ium* ib*ide*m q*uo*d null*us* tenens ib*ide*m ponat aliqua ani*mali*a in *communi*bus campis post*quam* seminat*i* fu*er*int quousq*ue* grana om*n*ia ex campis ill*is* sint asportat*a* Et etia*m* q*uo*d non impon*at* aliquos equos aut [1] al*ia* ani*mali*a nisi ligat*a*

pen*a* fu*er*int sub pen*a* cuiusl*ib*et vj^{s}viij^{d} Et [2]

affur*atores*	Joh*ann*es Waker	Jur*ati*
	Joh*ann*es liggerd	

Ext*racta* fiant [3] & deliber*ata* Ballio

1 alt*er*a cancelled.

2 q*uo*d non custod*iat* aliquos cancelled.

3 MS: fian*tur*.

(40^{d}), who have destroyed the grain of the tenants in the common fields there, remain in mercy as etc.. 1552

At this court it is ordered, both by the authority of this court and by the assent of all the tenants there, that no tenant there shall put any beasts in the common fields after they have been sown until all the grain from those fields has been carried away. And moreover, that they shall not put therein any horses or [1] other animals unless they have
Penalty been tethered, under a penalty for each and every one of them of 6^{s}8^{d}. And [2]

Affeerers	John Waker John Liggerd	Sworn

Let extracts be made and delivered to the bailiff.

Index

NOTE: References are given to the introduction only where this relates to entries in the roll.